Working Women of Somerset

Photographer Pauline Rook, a working woman of Somerset.
Picture by Denise Owen.

Working Women of Somerset

As told to James Crowden
with photographs by Pauline Rook

AGRE

First published in 2001
by AGRE BOOKS
Groom's Cottage, Nettlecombe, Bridport, Dorset, DT6 3SS
www.agrebooks.co.uk

Typeset by Agre Books, printed and bound by R. Booth Ltd, Mabe, Cornwall

ISBN 0 9538000 5 9
A CIP catalogue record for this book is available from the British Library

ACKNOWLEDGEMENTS

James Crowden and Pauline Rook would like to thank The Paul Hamlyn Foundation, South West Arts, South Somerset District Council and the Somerset Rural Life Museum in Glastonbury for supporting this publication. We would also like to thank: Somerset Now!, Mark Etherington, Jacy Wall, Barry Lane, Sue Isherwood, Jo Plimmer, David Walker, Bob Butler, Year of the Artist, Ron Frampton, and of course the women themselves for welcoming us into their homes.

WORKING WOMEN

Eileen Pittard, Landlady	6
Joy Thorne, Expenditor	10
Tracey Boyland, Cleaner and Massage Therapist	15
Fran Evens, Beef Farmer	17
Emma Taylor, Cidermaker	22
Sue Applegate, Cornet Player	27
Rosy Gray, Bookbinder	31
Judy Halfhide, Chef	34
Rosa Davis, Haberdasher	38
Sue Hasell, Vegetable Grower	42
Jennifer John, Chair Bottomer	46
Carolyn Perrin, Eel Filleter	51
Barbara Butler, Funeral Director	54
Jackie Smith, Groom	58
Jo Mouland, Radiographer	62
Gloria Fouracre, Lavatory Attendant	67
Nancy Walker, Vegetable Seller	70
Caroline Jackson, Hospice Nurse	73
Evelyn Body, Sculptor	79
Gill Samways, Farmer's Wife	82
Margaret Spencer, Rocking Horse Specialist	87
Nancy Berrey, Volunteer	90
Doris Pile, Matron	94
Elfrida Savigear, Rector	99
Wendy Suckling, Glover	103
June Small, Apple Grower	107
Pennie Hill, Ladies' Hat Hirer	111
Angie Allen, Painter and Decorator	115
Catherine Pike, Bloodhound Master	119
Sandra Pocock, Butcher	122

The pub has been in our family for over 130 years and has always passed down the female side. And before that it belonged to Biddie Masters, also a relative. It's known as Eli's after my father, who was licensee here fifty-five years. The sign which said Rose & Crown fell down one day, my mother didn't like the sign very much anyway, so for quite a while they didn't put it back up. It just came to be known as Eli's. His father was also called Eli. He died of pneumonia when my father was six weeks old. It was his dying wish that he should also be called Eli.

I was born on Friday the 13th of April, 1923, in the bedroom above where we are sitting now, that's the Men's Kitchen. My mother was born there and all my family were born there. My grandfather William Slade was a sitting tenant in the early 1900s and bought it off the Duke of Devonshire. William had three jobs, he was a farmer, a publican and a stonemason. Then the First World War came and both my uncles were killed. Sid was in the Somerset Light Infantry and Reg was a Sergeant in the Coldstream Guards. He went to France and was killed very soon. He was a good shot and liked swimming. Of course I never knew them but mother talked about them so much I felt as if I had grown up with them. That's their pictures on the wall up there. Reg is the one with the moustache. It hit my mother very badly and she couldn't bear to even go to the memorial services. Curiously enough my daughter Maureen was born on Armistice Day. Some people say my son Stephen looks just like Sid. I always used to sneak

into the Men's Kitchen to listen to them and one man would always bring in two pieces of homemade fruit cake. One for him and one for me. They sometimes brought their food in. Occasionally they would do bloaters over the fire with a toasting fork. Or else they got bread and cheese for 6d. At 6.30 in the morning they would pick up their cider flagons before going to work. Some were farmworkers and withy cutters, others worked at Kelway's Nursery or were gangers on the railway. They used to step-dance on the floor and Grandfather had to replace one of the flagstones that had got worn out with hobnails. And then they would sit around in a circle, one after the other. Sing, Say, Whistle or Pay... and if you didn't perform you had to pay for a round... Cecil Sharp, he collected a few songs around here. Cider was 3d a pint, beer 4d and best bitter 6d. Father would go round the farms sampling cider and one day he was very late back and mother was getting worried. Eventually he came in and I saw his friend Jobie flat out in the cart and said 'Dad's all right but Jobie's dead'. Of course he was only drunk.

And then we made our own cider in the cider house and the apples were crushed by horsepower, the horse going round and round on a long shaft. I used to love to go in there and take some juice, where the skittle alley is now. I still call it the cider house. Then there was Mark's grocery shop, you could get anything there but that's before my time. Tobacco was very strong in those days, Digger Shag and Black Beauty, and a few took snuff. But they seldom got really drunk, they knew how much they could take.

During the war we had American, Scottish and English troops. There was a detention barracks up the road and this was the nearest pub. Also I had to go round when they allocated evacuees, dropping them off one by one. One little boy he was called Lenny, a very big family all split up, so I got him back with two of his sisters and kept an eye on him. A loveable little rascal he was. Then I got a job in Langport as the first woman Local Fuel Overseer, supervising the rationing for the twenty-six villages that made up Langport Rural District. Aller, Babcary, Barrington, Barton St David, Beercrocombe, Charlton Mackerel, Curry Rivel, Curry Mallet, Drayton, Keinton Mandeville, Kingsdon, Fivehead, Langport, Muchelney, Puckington, Isle Brewers, Isle Abbots, Kingsbury Episcopi, Long Sutton, High Ham, Compton Dundon, Hambridge, Westport, Huish Episcopi, Somerton, Kingweston. I hope I haven't left any out. Mostly coal and paraffin. Each household was allowed thirty-four hundred-weight of coal and two tons of coke a year. In some villages without electric or gas I could use my discretion to give them more, and when there was flooding I got more coal to help them dry their houses out. Sometimes even the pub flooded and I have served beer in my wellingtons. We have no bar here, only a cellar with barrels... Rationing went out in about 1952.

'I've had a diet of drainage since I was a kid'
Joy Thorne – Expenditor, Muchelney

As an Expenditor I am the 'eyes and ears' of the Drainage Board, their person on the ground and on the water. I have to liaise between the Board and the landowners and there are several hundred of them. The Langport Drainage Board has seventeen members, some are landowners, but others are appointed by the district council. How much they each pay as drainage rates is done on acreage, according to how much of their land got covered in the highest flood of the 1870s. Other householders used to pay direct to the board, but that is now collected by the council. The drainage boards, and there are several of them, are independent but work closely with the Environment Agency who look after the main rivers and the various structures like weirs, main drains and pumping stations. I have eighty miles of waterway 'in view'. The Yeo up to Rimpton, the Isle up to Donyatt, and Parrett up to the A303. In these parts a fast-flowing ditch counts as a stream.

My job is really checking on water levels and dealing with day-to-day phone calls from farmers when they notice something unusual, like traffic cones thrown into Mill Brook in Martock one Saturday night. I had to fish them out from under a bridge. Then there was a car in a ditch, but as there was no body in it the police weren't interested. Often there is driftwood which gathers behind floodgates and I have to clear it, which isn't always easy. Sometimes there are whole trees that have been washed down.

As far as water levels are concerned I shut the inlets on December 1st and make sure the outlets are open. Then again on 1st April I open

the inlets, but last year, because it was so wet, I didn't open them until the middle of May. When it's flooded, I can't do much, as it is all under water more or less. Most of my work comes in the summer. Maybe eight to ten hours a week. If there's engineering work to be carried out, the engineer, Dan Alsop, normally lets me know and I have to fill out notices to the farmers giving them a week to move any animals, and then I check up on the contractors to see that they have done what they said they were going to do. In the summer there are quite a few Hymac's slews clearing ditches and rhines. It's an interesting job and gets me out in the middle of the day. I am the only woman Expenditor they've ever had but I was born on the levels at Almonry Farm. I put in for the job and I've had it for four years now. I took over from Clifford Mounter and he'd had it for twenty-six years. There was a three-month handover period because it was such an extensive area.

I stayed at Almonry for the first twenty-three years of my life until I got married. My father rented the farm. We had a corn mill in the barn, that was in the days of West of England sacks and it was useful after Thorney Mill packed up. Floods were bad... they stayed longer then, maybe six weeks or more because there were no pumping stations here till the Sixties and it would stink a bit. Nowadays the floods come up quicker because of all the extra drainage farmers have put in as well as the new building in towns. But there's less stock now than there used to be. The village still gets cut off. We did this Christmas. In 1990 it was for two weeks. We used to have cows who would walk through water to get to the kale and then come back at milking time of their own accord, we used to leave the gates open as there was no traffic and the water washed off the udders. Very clean they were. Down at Horsey Farm they would have to bring the milk over by boat and sometimes if there was a strong wind they would have to come up by the hedge and even break the ice if it froze. Then we'd take it up to the milk depot at Thorney. Sometimes we would pick up apples by boat.

After leaving Muchelney I went to Newport at Wrantage and then Hatch Beauchamp... bought a plot, then my husband built a bungalow. Then Ham Down between Langport and Somerton where we kept a beef suckler herd. I worked for my father and after he died we bought my mother and sisters out. I ran it on my own for five years, not easy getting cows across the main road. Then we moved here and did the house up and sold off the barn. I now do bed and breakfast and have two self-catering cottages.

Being an Expenditor fits in very well. After the bacon and eggs and changing beds I get my wellingtons on and drive around. When I put in for the job, I didn't think I'd get it, but as Richard England said 'I've had a diet of drainage since I was a kid,' so I was born to it in a way.

'There's even talk of French Romany'
Tracey Boyland - Cleaner and Sports Massage Therapist,
Winsham

My grandfather, my mother's father, was Robert Priddle. He owned the farm down at Hambridge, just past the old brewery on the bend by the bridge. He had all the fields down the bottom and also owned withy beds down on Westmoor. He went in with his brother-in-law, had a big falling out and eventually had to sell it all off. They never spoke again. Grandfather moved to Bridge Cottage and worked at the mill for Allied Breweries, now Chalon. He used to load up the beer onto the lorries and my dad worked there as well. He used to go to the pubs mending pumps. He was killed in a car accident coming back from the Bath & West. He was thirty-seven. I was eleven and my brother was eight. It was terrible.

My mother took a part time job in a shop in Langport. That must have been 1978.

I went to school at Huish and did a YTS scheme in hairdressing at Veronique's in Curry Rivel. I then did four years at Clark's shoe factory near Ilminster. I was a match marker, matching up the leather once it was cut for the sewing. Cowhide, lovely smell. Then I had Kelly, my first daughter. I couldn't work regular hours so I took a job at the Palace Nightclub in Crewkerne as a barmaid, three nights a week, 6pm till 3am.

I did that for two years. It was hard work, but the money came in handy and a bit of a social life. Many fights. Mostly between men. Too much drink and attitude problems. I enjoyed it. At that time I was living at Barrington and also did work as a homeworker for Burfield's of Martock sewing badges on golf gloves. I did that all in all for five years. I was a busy girl. I even worked in Leo's in Yeovil stacking shelves in the evenings to help pay for my wedding to Nick. Then I moved to Winsham and worked at Hornsbury Mills outside Chard in the gift shop and showing people round the mill, explaining how it all worked.

I also did the odd bit of cleaning work but there was no future in it, a bit of pin money really, so I went to college at Strode and did an ITEC Diploma in Anatomy, Physiology and Massage. I paid for the fees by doing demonstration and field-marketing work, mostly in supermarkets, getting customers to sample new products like cheese, coffee, biscuits, wine. Promotion work really. Then I did an NVQ2 beauty therapy and studied sports injury massage for six months. I am now freelance and the business is growing.

As to the family, I now have three children, Kelly, Natalie and Guy. My husband has a small garage in the village and builds motorcycle trikes which are selling well. My brother puts the smiling faces on the Henry Hoovers at Numatic in Chard.

Oh my looks, people always ask me where I am from, so I say Hambridge, but they don't believe me. All I know is that my father's sisters are still trying to sort out the family tree, as there is definitely 'foreign' blood in the family. One of them says Spanish and there's even talk of French Romany...

'The bullock ate her silk gloves'
Fran Evens - Beef Farmer, Ash Priors

It's not stubbornness, it's determination. I always get everything I want in the end. Take these ear tags, cruelty it is. That big and they just rip the ear. The Ministry in their wisdom. I stood my ground on that one.

Born? I was born in Chiswick, terrifically eccentric parents, with my father an Oxford Don, art, and my mother an Antique Dealer and restorer. She repaired murals in the British Museum. Very valuable, had to be locked in there, sometimes till nine at night.

As a child I used to take rabbits and chickens over to the common on a piece of string, till I got run over by a bus. I was about four or five. I can't have been very tall as the bus's bumper caught me in the back of the neck. So that was all stopped. We went on holiday to the Isle of Wight and I chucked everybody's coats and hats in the sea. 'Valerie, that child is mad,' my father used to say. During the war we went to Wales. That was another saga. Then there was East Anglia. A thatched house and a field. We'd have chickens, goats, and cheese. One day the goat broke the cloches, I got the blame. Then I went and broke all the remaining cloches. 'Valerie that child is mad.' The good life. Mother made bread you couldn't cut let alone eat. They'd read all the books. £6 a week. Selling eggs and cheese. Where could we buy a farm? £3,500, fifty-four acres, 1954, Exmoor. Of course we baled the first lot of hay at the wrong time. Neighbours must have had a chuckle. First cow got Johne's disease, shat everywhere, even sprayed it over the postman, got it in his bag, had to hose off the letters, course the ink

ran. Seven years on Exmoor, John and I, that's my husband, a farming contractor. Then he drowned in Portland bay, sailing accident. I drove home, four kids. I couldn't remember anything after that. Not for six months, just blanked it out. Six down to eleven months. One Saturday I came out of it. Odd. I then realised that I was in a man's world. I had to be tough.

My son went to Brymore and he came home. I made him walk back. That's a hell of a long way for an eleven-year-old. But he learnt his lesson. And then there were chores. Didn't feed him for days. That was another lesson. It's just like a bull. If you give in they get you next time. Came off Exmoor in 1971. Percy used to buy all the grass keep, P.H. we call him. He had two children. His wife had run off with the cowman. So I said I'd look after everybody if he'd pay the bills until the kids left school and then we'd split, but I am still with him after thirty years... that was last August.

He had 1,700 cattle, now he's semi-retired only got 900. We came to Green Acre, that's Ash Priors. Then started farming properly in '75. Paid £270 for a Charolais heifer. I knew when I saw her she was the right animal. I would go to London and watched shows and judging for five years. Any show anywhere. I'd get glued to them. I do. I can't take my eyes off them. Then I started showing. Champflower Charolais. Red and white banners, so people thought we'd won before we had. 1989 Smithfield. Met the Queen Mum. The bullock ate her silk gloves. Said she'd bring two pairs next year and she did. Got the Duke of Norfolk cup second year. First woman. They didn't like it.

And as for the stockman's quarters. They stay there for £28 a night in Kensington and I had to get a hotel for the week. £590. Used to get a lift down on a milkfloat. I was determined to stay there. Took my sleeping bag and wouldn't budge. They knew I meant business. First woman to stay there in 210 years. Now 100 women stay. I did very well showing. Five Supreme Champions. In '91 and '92 Champflower Bill. His semen gone all over the world. Even to India. Men don't like it. They wouldn't speak to me. Tried to get me out. It's character building. You must have identification, I had my ten-gallon hat as well. So they wouldn't forget me... I pulled out in 1992. Every animal I had taken was Supreme Champion. So that was that.

After Smithfield I met a fantastic man at the Royal Show, I don't know who he was. In two hours he told me everything he knew. Then there was the pen of Highland Cattle. Feet were very bad. 'I'd sack that stockman if they were mine,' I said. The man behind me said 'well actually they're mine'. He was Lord Guinness. He did sack his stockman and next year he gave me a cheque for £100. 'Best advice I've ever had,' he said.

Then I started getting involved in all sorts of issues. Eat this, eat that. Chairperson WFU, NFU PR Somerset. I love people. I love helping people. So much has happened to me. I have come through with a lot of help from people. Three years ago last January I organised a Farmers' Rally in Exeter. Six thousand farmers. Took three hours on the phone. And all for free. I twist people's arms.

Forty-five nursing cows, forty youngsters. I cull very hard. Last year a beast was worth only £200 because of the OTS scheme - Over Thirty Months. Now they are worth £800. My chaps weigh a ton. BSE cost me dear. Never had it. Farcical really. Only 100,000 in ten years. And this CJD. Why haven't slaughtermen got it? They get spinal fluid and bits all over them when they cut up carcasses. Maggot on the brain. That's what it was always called, it's nothing new. Farming won't pick up till 2006. Economists say we'll bump along. Subsidies should be for quality not quantity. Look at hill farmers. Should be on area not headage. In 1998 a cow was worth £1,200, now they're worth £400. Buy one, get two free. Fifty per cent of farmers are over fifty-eight. That means there's going to be a shortfall in a few years' time.

'Help Yourself Leaflets' and package. I've sent thousands out in the last five weeks. I just thought if I could stop one person from shooting themselves it would be worth it. Farmers are desperate and too proud to take benefits. People phone at night. Introduced it in Devon, Somerset and Cornwall. Now it's nationwide. It just took off. Working Families Tax and Credit benefits. They can do it by phone.

My mother? She died of a stroke. My father took his life six weeks later. She was in hospital and she heard the doctors saying 'she's not going to live very long,' she lasted six months. She died when he had gone. Her funeral was weird. No service or anything. You just couldn't believe it. No hymns, nobody said anything about Mother. And he was at her bedside nearly all the time. When he went he laid everything out on the table, Jaffa Cakes, biscuits, sherry and teapots, keys, bank statements. Meticulous really. New clothes. He'd been taught by Picasso at one time, left us nothing. Destroyed all his work and sculpture. Even Picasso drawings and prints. All went.

Accidents? Once got tossed by a bull, up and over, then against the wall, grabbed him by a nose ring for all I was worth, then scrambled out. Drove nine miles, my back covered in shit, legs black and blue, doctor said he'd never treated a live matador before.

'I swapped my wellies for stilettos and my waterproofs for a mini skirt and sequins'
Emma Taylor - Karaoke Singer, Cidermaker, Burrow Hill

I was born in Taunton in 1967. I lived with my mother, she did loads of different jobs, administrator for two old people's homes in Taunton, freelance catering, did the books on a dairy farm at Bishop's Hull, worked at the Brewhouse. Father was managing director of an advertising agency in Knightsbridge. When that ended he ran a pub in Devon. The Red Lion in Dittisham. My grandmother was Mayor's secretary in Taunton for twenty-five years.

I went to Taunton School, not that it shows now. Two years at Richard Huish. My first job was on Saturday as Dinner Lady at King's College. Really funny, my brother was a student there. He thought we were the lowest of the low. £1 an hour. I moved up to London, became a student. French and Spanish. I didn't get a degree, but I learnt a lot about life. Loads of jobs, in pubs, cleaning work. Even an office. One and only time. Horrendous. Eighteen women crammed in one room bitching away all day.

Then I left college, bought a truck, became a hippie. A fairly mild traveller. Mostly in Sussex on fruit farms, picking apples, beans, raspberries. On the road for six years. Then a chance to go back to college. I did an HNC in horticulture at Brinsbury College and that set me up. I came back to Somerset. Got a house in Bishops Lydeard and set up my gardening business. That went on for two years. Then I got a job at Cannington as a technician. I looked after all the outdoor nurseries. I learnt grafting, fruit trees, a few ornamentals and budding

roses. I was in charge of the propagation. I saved enough money to go overseas. Went travelling four months in India, then flew to Tokyo to make my fortune as a hostess in a karaoke bar. Three months. One hell of an experience for someone who has come from the countryside and worked outdoors. It involved a hell of a lot of compromise. I swapped my wellies for stilettos and my waterproofs for a mini skirt and sequins. Loads and loads of make-up. Every night I had to stand on the street looking like a hooker trying to encourage men to come in and drink and sing karaoke. There were hundreds of girls doing the same thing in Roppongi, the red light district. Sex clubs, strip clubs, casinos. Full on. They're obsessed with karaoke. Start at eight, didn't finish till about 3-4am. You had to chat them up. For a hundred dollars they got a bottle of whisky and a girl for an hour. They paid for your drinks. So we were paid to get pissed, but you had to keep it together. You had to stand up and dance, sing, be the life and soul of the party.

The Japanese work horrendous hours with a lot of pressure. Japanese women are not very outgoing. We used to sing Abba, Beatles. They are crazy about The Beatles. We were all western girls, a lot of English, most men's dreams. All blonde chicks, eighteen to twenty-eight. What a laugh. We had bouncers, burly Swedish blokes. If any of the men touched us they were out. They were completely rat-arsed. Outrageous. They came out of themselves. I earned 1,000 US dollars a week after expenses. Some of the girls had their own agenda but that was their concern. I never felt threatened. I lived in a minute flat with three other girls. I left after three months with 7,000 US dollars, then went on a very long holiday. Sri Lanka, Indonesia, Thailand, India. Then Australia where I worked for six months on a rose-budding contract, just outside Adelaide. Then back to the UK via Indonesia selling sarongs and jewellery at festivals and car boot sales. Then back to Australia up to Cairns. Beautiful. Eighty kilometres north. Port Douglas where I did landscaping and horticulture for two years. I also worked on a building site. The only woman with 100 blokes. The Aussies are very racist and sexist, so I had to keep up with them. They're not allowed to wolf-whistle, no pinching, no sexual harassment. After a while they respect you and you feel like one of the lads. I then went to New Zealand budding and grafting in the Bay of Plenty and then up to Keri Keri.

I came back this summer and got a job tractor-driving at Burrow Hill. Julian said 'they need a bit of crumpet in the cider house to keep morale levels high'. Whose morale I wondered? Here I have been building cheeses, pressing apples, making cider, keeping the troops entertained.

I will go back to New Zealand and work with one of the top rose breeders. The grass is always greener on the other side of the world. If you keep travelling, you keep finding work, you can do anything...

'Once I discovered cider I was well away'
Sue Applegate - Cows and Cornets, Burrow Hill

I was born in Oxford. Dad was in the RAF, a Flight Lieutenant flying Jet Provosts. We then went to Singapore and Germany, settling in Seavington St Michael in 1969. He then worked for Westland's as a quality control engineer. Right from the age of eight, I decided I wanted to milk cows, because there was a farm in the village with a house cow and the farmer would milk her with a three-legged stool. So that made me see something I had never seen before, the tranquillity, an ideal picture of what I wanted. Feet on the ground and working with large animals.

I went to school at Wadham in Crewkerne. They had a farm there. Twelve large white sows, three Anguses, some chickens and a tractor, an old 35. I remember bombing round the school car park on the tractor before school. I'd get there at 8.15, clean out the pigs every morning. Wadham had only been open three years and some of the farm buildings were left. The only subject I took an interest in was Rural Science. Farming was my rebellion. I've done it through determination.

As to the trumpet, that started at Swanmead in Ilminster when I was nine. I had my front teeth sticking out at right angles so the dentist Mr Cropper said that I either had to have a brace or start playing the trumpet. So it was my dentist who got me interested in playing the trumpet. The pressure of the mouthpiece was enough to do the trick. I joined the Kingsbury Episcopi band in 1973 aged eleven. One of four girls out of twenty-five to thirty men. All the old men drank cider, withy cutters, tanker drivers. Stories, lots of stories, entirely traditional. I was totally enthralled. It took about ten years to be accepted. Wedmore Harvest Home was always the best and everybody was wrecked. Teddy Hartland stood on his cornet and crumpled it like a milktop. Then there was Langport Club Day and Eli's. Once I discovered cider I was well away...

I now play the solos on the cornet... *Last Post* on Armistice Day. Modern pieces as well as traditional. I also play in the Wessex Military Band at Bridport. We've been to Sandhurst, the Albert Hall, Berlin and Hanover. The Germans love *Colonel Bogey*...

I left school at sixteen. Started at Scott's Nurseries Youth Training Scheme. They put me on all sorts of things but after two weeks I'd had enough of poncing around with plants. I wanted cows. I saw a job advertised at White Lackington and they put me in touch with John Down at Dowlish Wake. I got the job as student general farm worker at 75p an hour. One hundred and eighty cows. So I looked after the replacement calves and beef calves. Then in September 1980 I went to do an NCA at Cannington Agricultural College. Then I got a job at Frome milking a small dairy herd but I was living in a caravan. After eight weeks I came back to Lopen and worked there till July 1982. I did a week's potato picking for which I wasn't paid. Then to a farm shop at West Lambrook. Laid off on Christmas Eve. I heard there was possibly a job going at Darby's. Their herdsman of twenty-six years had retired. I didn't hear anything for a while and then Don phoned up. I started on January 3rd, 1983. They had 120 cows. Start at five in the morning, twelve days a fortnight. Finish at 9.30. Then the middle of the day off. Start again at three, finish at six. Stayed milking for three years. Then did a couple of A-Levels at SCAT. Geography and Environmental Studies. A friend of mine, Pat, took over the Darbys' milking, and so I could stay on in the cottage.

No responsibility without qualifications... and so I went to Seale-Hayne at Newton Abbot for an HND in agriculture. For the first time in my life I did quite well at academic work. Then I went on to do a degree in Agriculture and Countryside Management. When I left college I got a job with the Milk Marketing Board as a milk-recording supervisor, covering Frome, Shaftesbury and Yeovil. Twenty-five milk recorders and 250 farms. Sampling for butterfat, lactose, protein and the somatic cell count as a mastitis indicator. We had 250,000 samples to test everyday. And with having to do the shows it was too much.

I then took a job for two years at Cannington, organising practicals on their farm and various farms around, and helped with the Learning Support Department. One-to-one. I then went gardening on my own. In October '98 I saw a job advertised at Kelways for a Landperson. I got the job and now look after their tractors, the cultivation, spraying, harvesting and planting. Acres of peonies and irises... Last week I was chain-sawing willows...

'Sometimes a whole family will watch you for half an hour'
Rosy Gray - The Black Cat Bindery, Castle Cary

I was born in Bristol near the Italian Cafe in Clifton, round the corner
from a friend of ours called Nell, an opera singer who had taken tea
with Hitler. Then we moved on to the cut all round the Midlands and
hauled coal in narrow boats along the Grand Union Canal from
Ashby-de-la-Zouch to Camden Lock, selling it by the sack load door-
to-door. *Redshank* had the motor and *Greenshank* was the 'butty',
towed behind and connected by a long rope. They were both 72ft long,
7ft wide and built in the Thirties, each carrying twenty-five tons. The
colourful cramped back cabins were our only home for three years. I
nearly drowned in Camden Lock, before it became a trendy thing to
do. Luckily someone spotted me fall in and Mum dragged me out. I
was three.

My parents, Nick and Corinna, realising that coal was hard work,
decided to concentrate on self-loading cargo and started doing trips in
London. This was in the early Seventies. They then returned to Bristol
Docks and started the *Bristol Packet* on Wapping Wharf next to the
Great Britain. There were school trips, trips upriver to Beese's tea
gardens, booze cruises and even trips all the way up to Bath. The legal
capacity was fifty-four. It was so successful that we bought another
vessel called the *Tower Belle* which had worked on the Thames and
carried 120. She had started life in 1920 on the Tyne carrying shipyard
workers. The *Tower Belle* also did trips down the Avon Gorge which
was very spectacular. I would often come straight from school and be
expected to work the bar or act as crew. One week I earned £80, which

was a lot of money in those days for someone under twelve. But as we were offshore Dad said that it didn't matter. The licensing laws didn't apply either. My parents did that for six years till 1980 and then sold up. The business is still running today, though the docks have changed, the warehouses have all been converted and the sand dredgers have gone.

After that I went to live with my mother near Shaftesbury in Dorset. Dad went on the canals in France, and Henry, my brother, went to sea aged sixteen and worked on small coasters. I went to Bournemouth Art College and then travelled to South America and India before being offered a job at a bindery called Collis-Bird & Withey in Holloway when I was nineteen. I worked there for a year and then went to the London College of Printing for a two-year course. After that I joined two friends and helped set up the Wyvern Bindery in Clerkenwell. I was there ten years and did a large number of jobs including work for Linda McCartney and Aston Martin. We bound Bram Stoker's *Frankenstein Diaries*, *The English Patient* and photographs for a rave band called KLF who burnt a suitcase containing £1M, they also took a cardboard cut-out to the North Pole. At the moment we are waiting to bind a limited edition of *Tiger's Bride* by Angela Carter.

Our shop has a large curved window and it's a bit like being in a goldfish bowl. A lot of people don't know what bookbinding entails as most binders have workshops tucked away. In a sense it is free advertising but you feel odd even sitting down for a cup of tea. Sometimes a whole family will watch you for half an hour. There is always a hardcore of people who will want work done and we regularly do work for one international book dealer in London. The art of bookbinding is very ancient and predates the invention of printing by at least 500 years. Most of the leather is Nigerian goatskin though we do use cowhide, vellum, wooden boards, snakeskin and we even have skate skin. Some possum skins are on their way from New Zealand. Possums are a real pest over there. They are tanned with tea tree bark. The leather is cut with a scalpel.

Often we have to do all sorts of repair work, even matching up marbled end papers. These we get from Anne Muir just outside Frome. She uses carragheen and water rather than oil. All of the bookbinding work has to be done very precisely. We sew books in section with waxed cotton thread. Most of our machinery is Victorian. The star-backer was made in 1851. We have to forward the book, make the spines, finish the cover, which can often involve gold tooling, provide silk headbands, and sometimes a presentation box. We have a finishing press, a guillotine and a glue pot... In the photograph I am working on an accounts book. I realise I couldn't work for anybody else. I like the independence.

The baby's due in four weeks...

'Some like it hot'
Judy Halfhide - Chef, Yeovil Fire Station

I started working as a very cheaply paid waitress in Milborne Port aged about fifteen... they kept us up till 1am. Then I went for a career as a Reconnaissance Photographer in the RAF and I had to get fit for that. During the training I met my future husband and I started working for him as a secretary. He was a property developer in and around Yeovil. Large houses, large estates and some sheltered housing schemes, one just up the road from The Black Horse pub. I was eighteen, he was twenty-two. He sent me to college doing secretarial and business studies. I turned the RAF down. I had fallen in love...

I then got married, had two children. The recession made a drastic change in our lives, so I had to help out in some way. It was desperate at home. I did cleaning up the road, the mortgage was heavy and my husband needed help. I had to pay someone to look after my son. I earned pence... pre-school was very difficult. I needed to earn more, so I took a job at Yeovil Hospital as a cleaner. The pay was good, £4.79 an hour, but I found it a difficult place to work, it was very hard to break the ice. I ended up in the Physio ward doing pencil portraits of their children. That's when the art side picked up. I would sell portraits every year. I've even done book illustrations for a children's book my husband wrote.

Then I got a job at the NAAFI in Yeovilton in the kitchens. I was very, very shy and very afraid. The chef always made out that he was very clever and would set me challenges like seeing who could cut up a cucumber into the most slices in the least time. He did 100. I did 150...

I was there about a year and a half. It was the thrill of seeing Prince Andrew take my food, that was a real turning point. Then I realised that I loved catering. He used to call in quite often as he was a helicopter pilot.

After that I did an intensive Catering and Chef's course at The Carpenter's Arms in Chilthorne Domer. It was very, very hard... long gruelling hours. I wanted to be a buffet chef, I enjoyed the events and the social occasions. I loved being faster, having new ideas. People taking photographs of your food is the best compliment. Producing food that looks good and tastes good is as big a thrill as painting a really good picture. There is nothing like that feeling when people come into a room, see your food and take a deep breath.

After two years at The Carpenter's Arms I phoned up a job agency. They were desperate for a chef. I had to feed about eight people and the hours were nine to three. Perfect for school. It was the Fire Station. I took a big gulp when I rang the doorbell, lots of knee-knocking. I was shown around the Fire Station and decided to throw myself in at the deep end or be a coward for the rest of my life. The first day I was very nervous. They all lined up to attention and I ran past them up the stairs to the kitchen.

The day-to-day routine is to give the Fire Prevention Officers tea at nine o'clock. Then I get orders for the day. Rolls at 11am and in between times I will have done the shopping. I jog down to the supermarket. They pay me for the food. They say what they want and give me the money. I have occasionally suggested rolled badger for Blue Watch as it saved them money. They would definitely eat it... They hate vegetables and I've witnessed some fantastic food fights. I love them really. Green Watch pictured with me are the gourmet watch. They like good food, even nouveau cuisine and pay me well. Even £5 each. You have to be very punctual.

Lunch at 1pm. If the alarm goes off when they are eating I have to make a map of where they are sitting, number each plate and keep it hot in the hot plate. You can't keep food for more than two hours like that. Then you ditch it. When the alarm does go off there's lots of sirens and whoops of excitement as they slide down the pole - others run down the stairs. Then it goes quiet.

When they return they try to be happy, to take their mind off things, watch television - road traffic accidents are the worst. Sometimes two or three a day. They have to deal with mangled bodies. They have to have great strength when they come back. Sometimes they are very, very quiet. My role is to be normal and pretend nothing has happened. There are four watches - Blue, Green, White and Red. They do two days on, 9am to 6pm, then two nights 6pm to 9am, then four days off. They sleep in their clothes. They are the cream of the country and I love them.

'People feel at home here'
Rosa Davis - Miss Dyer - The Draper's Daughter, Ilminster

Ilminster, no place like it. I love it. My father, Richard Dyer, bought
the shop in 1937 from Bob Wheadon, whose father had started the
business in 1870, they had their diamond jubilee in 1930. The name
R.P. Wheadon is still engraved on the glass doors and in the mosaic on
the floor. He used to milk cows, pedigree Jerseys, and would sell
cream and milk. Some of the outbuildings are still called the Dairy
and the Coach House. He even raised swans and white peacocks
which he used to sell abroad. So the Wheadons were here for sixty-
seven years and we've been here ever since. Father had a small shop
in Bristol and before that he lived in Shrewsbury in Shropshire.

I was two when he bought the shop, so we've been here sixty-three
years. I've been involved in the shop since I left school. People feel at
home here, they settle in right away. We have kept things in keeping.
People don't like it if we move anything, even a duster. They like it to
be just as they remembered it the last time they were here. My father
was very popular in the business, a real gentleman, always willing to
help people out, particularly when there was rationing. People would
often come here before they got married and choose their clothes, the
hats, the gloves, the shoes, the shirts, the dresses, the curtains, the
furniture, the bedding, everything apart from the kitchen sink. He
would be so patient with people and sometimes opened unofficially
after hours so that young couples could choose what they wanted.
Later, when they moved house, I would sometimes be left looking after
the baby while they went round the shop. We only lived next door so it

was very convenient. Nothing was too much trouble for Father, and if he didn't have something he would even offer to drive people to another town to get it.

In the early Sixties my father brought the Plaza, the old cinema next door, and it became a furniture showroom. My brother Bob was brilliant at carpet fitting and the other brother Tony was Brain of Britain and then Brain of Brains, but they wanted to do something different, so it was left to me to run the business, which I do to this day with my husband. He also does the bookkeeping. We employ thirteen staff most of whom are part-time, and some of them have been here nearly all their lives, they are very loyal and always come back. It's not just me, it's the place, people feel at home here, they have time to look, and we get very involved with our customers, they tell us everything, in strict confidence of course, the happy bits and the sad bits, it's lovely. When you go to their homes they show you their nice bits of furniture or their embroidery. They like the continuity, it's very important. Why someone phoned me up the other day...

'Is that Dyer's?'
'Yes.'
'Do you still keep underwear?'
'Yes.'
'Do you still keep men's underwear?'
'Yes.'
'Do you still keep string vests?'
'Yes.'
'Praise the Lord,' she said...

Some shops have music on, but we don't, it interrupts the gossip. We may seem old-fashioned, but things still go on approval in a brown paper bag. The bags still have our name on in the corner and are made in Plymouth. I do have a metre rule but I keep it hidden. Cards? No we don't take cards, just good old-fashioned money and cheques.

Nowadays we have to carry so much more stock. Everything has to be colour co-ordinated. In the old days there were only two sorts of sheets, cotton and flannelette and only two sizes, single and double, now there's king size... Then there's duvets, with all the different togs and we still sell woollen blankets. Nothing wrong with natural fibres, the best by far. The last set of linen sheets I sold were £120 and I had to send away for them and they were only single size.

Upstairs we have ladies' dresses, bottle green sweatshirts, navy cardigans, all sorts of children's clothes... all sorts of hats... All the labels are sewn on by hand and all the receipts are still written out. The shop is up for sale. We have had several people interested, we just hope someone will come along and keep it going. It would be very sad if it all went...

'I always loved growing things'
Sue Hasell - Vegetable Grower, Lopen Head

I was brought up on a farm in the Chew Valley, which is near Bristol. It was a family farm. My grandfather, he had a farm in the Lake before it was dammed. Spring Farm, a beautiful place, wonderful, Elizabethan, the door on it, a huge studded oak door. The Lake was opened in 1956... all we've got now is photographs. My grandfather William was a forward-thinking farmer and he would move from one farm to another. He had four sons, my dad was the eldest. He bought his own farm and then bought up land between Chew Stoke and Chew Magna till he had about 200 acres. Dairy, it was all dairy then, but now there's very few dairy hands left.

I have always worked. I am an outdoor person, out with Dad on the farm. I used to milk on a Sunday with him and used to have a horse, because the land was split, a two mile walk across the dam. I used to bring the cows back on horseback, very often this used to coincide with mushroom picking, great big horse mushrooms, so we'd have a huge fried breakfast. I loved being on farms. I never found a farmer to marry... but I always loved growing things, I had a job in the village pricking out at 6d an hour. At fourteen I started experimenting with growing stuff and put it out on the roadside. I love seeing something come to life. School was appalling... no careers advice. A convent... Then I did some boring jobs like secretarial. Hated it. Worked briefly in the office of a delphinium firm.

I bought a cottage at Oakhill. People were just beginning to move out of Bristol then. It wasn't until I was twenty-five that I retrained

and went to London to become a Youth and Community Worker. I was in London seven years. Putney. I loved London. So challenged by it. It brought out loads of issues I wanted to confront, so it was a very good time. Mostly local authority work, Wandsworth. Lots of different part-time jobs, the whole range, toddlers to pensioners. Set up loads of groups, then there was outdoor pursuits, canoeing, mountaineering... I just loved it. I am quite good at getting things off the ground. What I like doing is getting people to do what they want to do. I had a ball...

Both of us wanted to bring up our children in the country and that meant returning to Somerset, which was great... when I came back I found a lovely house in Chiselborough. New house, new baby... the growing thing. Part-time local Youth Worker with special needs students at Lufton Manor College, then I started growing and retailing dried flowers, traded with loads of florists. Late Eighties... early Nineties. I was the last allotment holder, you had to have four so I took on four, it was a great shame the village didn't buy it off the county council. It would have made an excellent play area for young kids.

After that I moved the growing to Little Norton. Had that for three years until I bought The Trading Post, which was an old filling station on the old A303. Four and a half acres. So really we took it on as a big challenge at the age of Christ knows what... I was beginning to wonder this morning... paperwork, shopwork. I just don't like being indoors. Steve is an excellent horticulturist. I have always liked doing different things but this is the biggest thing I have ever done. My perception at the beginning was that we would be growing - and just doing a box scheme - but there was great customer demand for organic food. The shop became viable within a few months. Lots of villages don't have village shops and ours became ridiculously busy. Our produce is grown without chemicals and pesticides, we follow all the guidelines and philosophies of the Soil Association but the grants dried up when we were applying. A lot of people prefer this road to the Ilminster bypass. Parking is very easy. We have an off-licence now and if we can't buy organic we buy local. Fresh bread, wholefood, Fair Trade teas and coffees, local cider, Combe Farm dairy products, a garden nursery, cut flowers. I get local people to make pasties and cakes, and we like to employ local people and take students from Lufton Manor College as well. Hopefully next year we can open a cafe in an old railway carriage that came from Leicester Railway Museum... Third Class... 1887.

I've had a good life so far. Just put up a new perimeter fence, £2,500. Bloody bunnies... you'd have thought it was for buffaloes.

'If you're in a rush, I'll cane your seat'
Jennifer John - Chair Bottomer, Stoke St Gregory

I was born in Hampshire. Shedfield, 1933. My father was a butcher, not an abattoir butcher but a family butcher. Five of us. I was the youngest. The business belonged to an aunt so we were a household of nine. Auntie Violet ran the Post Office. It was also a grocer's shop so it was the hub of the village. When the war came we could see Southampton and Portsmouth getting bombed. They used to come out in coachloads at night and sleep in the Reading Room. Mother used to make soup for them. Then we had evacuees in the house. On the Shedfield common there were gun emplacements. The nearest bomb was a quarter of a mile away and that did kill someone, then there were the incendiaries. All a bit exciting. Not a shelter really but a dugout. It smelt revolting, damp soil and slugs. Auntie Em refused to go down there and huddled under the piano.

I spent most of my holidays at my aunt's farm at Donhead St Andrew. A small mixed farm. I learned to hand milk, look after chickens and pigs. I still love cows now. I left school at sixteen and went to Sparsholt Farm Institute to do dairying. That was 1949. Just had fun... Girls were vastly out-numbered, three to one.

After Sparsholt I went to run a small herd of Guernseys at Eastleigh. Then I got married, that was 1954. We moved to an arable farm in West Sussex. My husband was a tractor driver. We met at Winchester Young Farmers... I did the calf rearing. Then we moved back to Hampshire and set up a relief milking business, which was a good idea. David had a van and I had a motorbike. It always broke

down and I was always being brought home in the back of lorries. We did that for three years and then a lady lent us some money to buy a smallholding of eleven acres. But we couldn't make any money at it. We had a pedigree cow to start us off, some pigs, Landrace and Large White as well as deep litter chickens. We kept that till we ran out of money. I had two children by this time, so that put the mockers on that.

David got a job with an animal feed company and we found a bungalow that we did up. Then moved on to an old farmhouse which we never finished. Both my daughters regard that as home. We were there from 1964. Husband ended up as Director of Animal Feeds. I worked there organising reps' calls but David died in 1981. Jaundiced. Cancer of the bile duct. He was only forty-nine.

I ended up selling the house because the daughters wouldn't leave home... I also had a job working with an Agricultural Chemistry Laboratory, nutritional analysis of feed. Mainly silage. Then I took a part-time job at Hampshire Farm Museum.

I always wanted to move west and found a cottage in Ilton. It was a super little village and I stayed there till '96. The noise of the Ilminster bypass was horrendous... a wall of sound, and then there were helicopters and low flying jets. I felt like shooting them down. For twenty years I had dabbled in antiques. Lifting didn't do my back any good, so I started on chairs and I've done that ever since. The rushes came from Philip Gears who had Turkey Cottage and he asked me if I'd be interested in getting my own rushes from the River Isle. There's quite a band of rush gatherers. We are after the bulrush not reedmace. It has a feathery head. We cut it with a sickle under water, and the sickle is always tied to your wrist. I prefer to get in the river. Shove on old clothes. We cut a stand every two years. Sometimes they are 8ft long and in a hot summer you can get sunburnt. Others cut from a boat. We handle them with care. Lie them out on the bank and sort through them, size them up and count the bundles, and divide by the number of helpers. In a good day we will get ten bundles each. Then you dry them out in your sheds. You have to keep turning them and sorting them. When they first come in it's a wonderful smell. Then when they are dry you wet them again, it's like a piece of rope. Very strong. Sometimes I mix in burr reed. Others use rush from Holland or Portugal, but it's harder to work. The cane, the rattan, comes from the Far East.

Nearly all repairs these days. You start in one corner and do a figure of eight, always working into the middle. I have a shell bodkin, side clippers and an old screwdriver for the cane and for the rush I use my hands and the handle of an old trowel to shove the off-cuts into the seat... People are much more appreciative of things done by hand these days... I do find chairs interesting. It's not materials it's time that matters... Rush hour... If you're in a rush, I'll cane your seat.

'They haven't escaped yet'
Carolyn Perrin - Eel Filleter, Lower Burrow

I were born in Doncaster and that's where I grew up. My father worked at a wire drawing factory. British Ropes. The Humber Bridge kept that company going. My mum always stood the market, sold sweets, homemade humbugs, mint fish, lemon drops. Always dressed like an Eskimo in winter. She loved the market, the hubbub. I do too. Both sets of grandparents came from the North East. Grandfather, Sailor Jim, he were in the Navy and Father was in the Navy. He was on decoy convoys. It's not something he ever talked about. My great-grandfather worked on the railways and got his leg caught between two carriages. Gangrene set in and that were the end of him. That's at Beamish where they got that reconstructed village.

When I was fourteen I used to stand the market. Since I was six, in fact, a fruit stall, shouting 'Shilling Pound Bananas'. The old lady Marjorie, she thought I was cute, and would sell more. I also worked on a farm, every Friday evening and Saturday. He had a green Morris Commercial open-back lorry, a fruit and veg round. I loved that. I used to go door-to-door. On frosty nights the metal scoop would stick to your hands. We wore Steptoe fingerless mitts. I started to drive the lorry when I was seventeen. Put L plates on, double de-clutching. Who needs a Ford Fiesta...

At sixteen I worked as a Post Room Clerk for British Ropes. Running around all day filling pigeon holes, collecting telexes. A year I lasted. I looked round and it was either the typing pool or accounts. Looking in vanity mirrors and painting nails. No thank you. So I went to the careers office. I think I favoured the Navy because of Dad and Granddad. Seventeen. I thought it would all be Hong Kong and assault courses, but it wasn't like that at all. Plymouth, Portsmouth and Yeovilton. Basic training at HMS *Raleigh*, Trooping. Five weeks. Hard but that was fun. Exciting. What I had gone looking for. So from there I did my trade training which is Air Engineering. HMS *Daedelus*. Wessex 5. Troop carriers. I was Radio Mechanic. I wanted to be a grubber, hands on. But if you grasped maths you were either weapons electrical or radio. I really didn't like it. Nothing to see. Just changing little black boxes. I came back to Yeovilton, 707 Squadron. Wrens' quarters were quite appalling, used to flood, running round with sandbags. You used to have to put everything on your bed. Three of us rented a cottage in Kingsbury Episcopi. A farm cottage, which brings me on to the marriage. That's how I met Steve. He used to pass by, then one day he left a big bunch of carrots and a swede on the kitchen table, all home grown. No flowers, no chocolates, just an invitation to Taunton Market. We were married in ten months.

I then left the Navy, did charity work, WRVS Langport. Numerous odd jobs. Delivering cars for John Yandle took me all over. Then John Chant's bakery at Bower Hinton with a bread round. Five mornings a week. Then when the children Samantha and Amber came I worked at home on the farm. Beef, sheep, arable. Pure Herefords. Eighty acres, flood regular. In 1992 started a riding school. That worked for quite a few years, fifty children a week. But everything was so expensive. Five ponies. I found it difficult with school hours so I gave it up and got three part-time jobs. Martock Co-op two mornings a week, East Lambrook The Rose & Crown, waitressing three evenings a week, then a paper round. Eight thousand papers a week. Delivering to paperboys and girls. I always have to fit in with the farm, keep the books up together, paperwork on the beef. This farm is too big for one but not big enough for two. I tried shift work at a food factory putting frozen strawberries and raspberries into yogurts on a conveyor belt. I felt seasick and brain dead. Then nursing home cleaning. At least you could talk to someone. Then delivering school meals. I did that for a year until Michael Brown at the Eel Smokery phoned me up. Really flexible hours, near to home. I love it out there. My role is eel filleter. The eels are smoked whole and filleted down to 4oz and 8oz packs. First you cut the head off and then run a sharp knife down each side of the spine, then cut down to board length and vacuum pack. I also go out and pick up live eels from the eel traps. They only run when there is no moon. Sometimes we pick up 500 kilos a week. That's half a ton of live eel. They haven't escaped yet... A few hairy moments... I also do bee-keeping and play trombone in the Kingsbury band.

'People sometimes buy their coffins in advance'
Barbara Butler - Funeral Director, Watchet

I was born in the middle of Sherwood Forest in 1929 in Nottinghamshire but lived in a small coal-mining village during the Depression. It was rough, kids came to school with holes in their shoes. I was a child of the Manse. My father was a Church of England vicar. Once you have been brought up in the country you are never shot of it. I went up to Oxford in the Forties to read English at Lady Margaret Hall. I had one of the last scholarships. There was still rationing. A bucket of coal a week. I then worked in an art gallery in Derbyshire. After a course at Bristol University I went to Kirkby in Liverpool as a social worker. *Z Cars* country. I taught at Bristol University for seven years. Then to London. Family case work at the Tavistock Clinic, then to Bedford College. I also did Jungian training in the Sixties. A pretty tough programme. Sixty hours a week, patients of both sorts. Quite a penance really. Then I worked at the Home Office in the Child Care Inspectorate, developing training. Then Brunel University to devise the first Master's programme in Social Work. Then to Cardiff where I was Director of the School of Social Work, then shifted over to Psychotherapy. I retired from academic work in the late Seventies but continued with analytic work. I was a founder member of the Severnside Institute for Psychotherapy. I am, I suppose, an originator, a pioneer. I moved to Watchet in 1989.

My mother had a series of severe strokes in the Eighties and was semi-paralysed. I looked after her here. What got me into funerals was total rage. We were told that my mother was dying. I wanted to find

out more about funeral arrangements. Getting factual information was very difficult from funeral directors. They only gave you an overall figure for a package deal. I did some research. Mother got better so when she actually did die I had the information to hand. I contacted coffin makers direct and took her to Taunton Deane Crematorium in the back of the Passat Estate car. I arranged it myself. Someone else drove. The staff were very good. You can even take the body home from the hospital if you want, so long as you have got the certificate. If people can handle it, it is just so real, and in a sense what I am doing now ties in with my Jungian analytical work. Involvement helps the grieving process.

That was in 1992. Quite a lot of people were intrigued that I had done it all myself and started asking me questions. Some even wanted to borrow the estate car. I opened a little shop in Williton called the One Stop Funeral Shop. People could come and see coffins and bits and pieces. This was about the same time as the Natural Death Centre opened in London. There was a great movement towards DIY funerals and woodland burial grounds.

Then people started saying - can you help us carry out the funerals? What is interesting is a local piece of ground appeared at the same time. The lady there set aside an acre, a couple of miles out of Watchet. It is private and people can consecrate bits if they want to. It's separate, perfectly legal and all official. There is a genuine response. I set up in 1994 and the business came to Watchet in 1995. It was a doctor's surgery so there was no real problem with change of use. We will do whatever people want. 'Funerals of your choice'. We try to open up to people. There is great flexibility. We can offer willow coffins and even have an all women's team called Martha's Funerals. We do about seventy funerals a year, but give a lot of free advice over the phone to people all over the country. It's rounding things off. People are now more willing to talk about death and dying. I think Diana opened things up but they were of course also tapping into their own personal grief in a public way. Sometimes I give talks to Women's Institutes and they think I am sizing them up.

You can bury somebody in pretty well anything so long as it's not metal or plastic. It has to be biodegradable for a woodland site. Cardboard coffins can take a body weighing sixteen to eighteen stone. They are quite strong really. People sometimes buy their coffins in advance.

I'll carry on as long as it takes. I would hate for it to become purely a commercial venture. It's only in the last decade or so that women funeral directors have come in. The antipathy towards women was very strong. You still get people who want a top hat. I usually wear navy or black. We had one funeral with balloons in Glastonbury. Most people don't believe in an after-life now. When you're dead you're gone...
I shall wait and see.

'When they race I can't bear to watch'
Jackie Smith - Groom, Woolminstone

I was born on Shiremoor Hill, in Merriott. Grandfather used to give me cider when I was a baby, he'd put it in my bottle to make me go to sleep. Then when I was two he bought me a pony and I've been in the saddle ever since. He was a market gardener and grew cabbages, potatoes and carrots, and had a round at Bridport and at Yeovil. He used to supply Gundry's canteen. We would often jump over jumps made from pea haulm. Both my father and mother worked at Scott's Nurseries. My father did landscape gardening and drove the lorries. He then went to Westland's. My mother stayed there and worked, in all, about twenty years. She was very good at pricking out. I never had a riding lesson in my life and Dad says I didn't cost him anything.

When I was at school I used to get off every second Tuesday in the month and go off to the pony sales in Exeter with my grandfather. So I had no education to speak of. Never had the same pony two years running. My grandfather was always buying and selling. I learnt most of it from him. Every weekend throughout the summer we'd go to shows. Gymkhana games and the jumping I enjoyed most. When I left school I went to work for Weyrad Electronics in Crewkerne. Making up circuit boards and transformers. I lasted there about five years. I worked part-time so that I could ride before I went to work.

I was twenty-one when my grandfather died. For a while I turned my back on the horses and then my sister saw an advert in *The County Mail*. Someone to help with point-to-pointers and hunters in Misterton. Mr Southcombe's. I worked there on and off for twenty

years. They had five horses on average. Mr Southcombe would muck the horses out and feed them by seven o'clock, still does now, must be therapeutic. And then I would ride them out with Frances, that's Mrs Southcombe, then wash them off and groom them. We'd go out in all weathers. An hour each one. And then rush home, wash and groom my two children. That job lasted September to May then I would go and help Dick Fawlston at his stud in Hardington preparing yearlings for sales. Newmarket. Five hours in a lorry. Away for a week. That's in October. I worked there on and off for ten years. I now work for Nigel Hawke who married Sophie Newman. They have a mixed yard of racehorses. Sophie has her own yard. If the horses need breaking-in we send them down there and get them back when they're educated. There's thirty there, at Woolminstone. I work round school hours, nine till 3.45 six days a week. It's never dull. It's always exciting. When you get up in the morning you never know what's going to happen

When they race I can't bear to watch but I do listen to the commentary. Last weekend I went off racing with my husband. First time in nineteen years. We had two jockeys ride for us. Tony McCoy at Market Rasen and Barry Keniry at Southwell. The horses I work with, you get to know them intimately. I care for them and over the years you get to know them very well. But I couldn't have done any of it without the help of my mother and father, and my husband was very supportive and easy-going.

The house I'm in now at Merriottsford, we've been here fifteen years. And it does flood. Up to the work-surface level in the kitchen. A bag of dog food broke open and plimmed up. It was everywhere. You need patience in this house. We don't have expensive furniture, there's no point. Once when I was up at Newmarket the Fire Brigade had to rescue my children. There was 2ft of water everywhere. Once it was four days before Christmas and the tree was afloat with its lights on. That was eleven years ago. And the animals, we just get them out of the way. We've got everything here. Dogs, ferrets, ponies, sheep, chickens, geese. One year all my rosettes got washed away down the river. We recovered them in a bag but the cardboard backings had all gone soggy. There were so many and my mother had written on all of them where I had won them. Sad really. Carpets you can replace but those, you can't. This autumn has been very wet, 2ft of water in the house four times, but life goes on.

Of course, I'll keep on riding as long as I can. Tim, that's my husband, says when I can't get in the saddle and get too grumpy stuck at home, he'll take me to a corner of a nice field and shoot me just like a racehorse. That's the kindest thing.

'The last few years it has been very, very hard work '
Jo Mouland - Sheep Shearing Contractor's Wife and
Radiographer, South Chard

I was born in Salisbury and brought up in Fordingbridge. My father was a bank manager. I trained as a Radiographer, met Mike at Young Farmers when I was fifteen and that was it really. He was a Shepherd at Whitsbury and he was dedicated then.

I went to Poole General, got married, lived in Verwood. Mike then went contracting with Billy Kinghorn... against his Dad's wishes... which meant shearing, fleece-rolling, dipping, crutching, foot-paring... all the dirty jobs. I used to go fleece-rolling for nothing till I got wise. Billy was a bit of a cowboy... shearers used to come and sleep on our floors because the contractor's caravans were so basic, there wasn't even glass in the windows. No showers, no food, nothing. So we used to take them in. That's where it all started.

That lasted nine months then Mike got a job down here as a Shepherd at Avishayes. We were there three years and then we were offered a small piece of land at Forton, thirty acres belonging to an old farmer called Mr Hocken. Mike had always helped him out with odd jobs. Then we moved to South Chard and bought a house on a new housing estate.

I used to work full-time in Taunton as a Radiographer to pay the mortgage and support Mike while he set up his contracting business. I operated the x-ray machines. I was a basic grade and did anything and everything. We had to be careful. What with radiation, sheep dip and shearers, it's a dangerous life. Now I do ultrasound most of the

time. Much safer. In that first year when Mike set up, we bought old ewes because that was all we could afford, the cheapest you could get. We've now gone from thirty acres to 400 and still use extra grass keep in the winter for 1,000 sheep and 150 head of cattle. The contracting business took off very quickly. We started shearing 2,000, and now shear 40,000. We have trailers for everything. Shearing, dipping, showering, jetting, foot-paring. We started with one Kiwi called Brent and he lived in our spare room for six weeks. Now we have up to anything from six to eight shearers and up to four 'rousers' - girls who roll the wool. Mostly Kiwis but some are Aussies.

My main job at shearing is to feed this lot three times a day for two months, as well as my family. I do their washing, post letters, make phone calls, pop to the shop, book airline tickets... Two of them have four eggs every morning, a big fry up and I do them packed lunches the evening before, I'm often working till midnight - sandwiches, rolls, pasties, cake, fruit. Some have strange eating habits. They don't like pork pies unless they are heated. I have never had a veggie shearer. I don't think they'd stand the pace. Everything has to be meat. They pay me £8 a day and that just about covers the food. They do their own drinks... cider with lager. And then there's the cooked meal in the evening with pudding. Children first. I've got four boys, Richard, James, Nick and Sam. The shearers in the picture are from left to right. Baldrick, Wayne, Pete and Trev. That's Mike in the middle.

I still do two days a week radiography over the hills to Taunton. A lovely drive. I joke with them there that I go to work for a rest. At least I get a lunch hour. I do all the bookwork on the farm. I also do most of the checking of the sheep and feeding the calves during shearing, as the gangs are out all hours, particularly if they're shearing far away. I am normally up at six. Then there's the meat which I market directly to the public through Somerset Food Links as Mouland's Meat.

The last few years it has been very, very hard work for not a lot of return. Many farmers had it too good for too long. We've always worked seven days a week for the last fifteen years. Family holiday? One week a year if you are lucky. Somebody still has to work every day. At least we didn't borrow large sums and buy a farm. We are in effect running a medium-size farm and a large contracting business from a housing estate. We have brilliant neighbours, we couldn't have survived without them. They've had the children at the strangest of times. Sometimes at two in the morning when we've had to go out night-lambing or calving. That's one of the reasons we don't want to move. We go to work like everyone else. Farming is very male-orientated...

I could do with a little more help in the kitchen and having a shearing trailer parked on your front lawn every night isn't ideal.

'I get husbands dragged in just to see the flowers'
Gloria Fouracre - Ladies' Lavatory Attendant, Taunton

I work four days a week. Monday, Tuesday, Fridays and Saturdays. I get a mid-week break. You need it to catch up on your own work. I cleaned the brass handles this morning. They don't shine the same in some weathers. I am going into my eleventh year here. You are always cleaning toilets. I've worked in hospitals - at Williton - a domestic there eight years and at Halcon Corner physically handicapped. I would say six years. Then I went part time at SCAT. Had to be there first thing in the morning, 6am.

I live at Norton Fitzwarren. Monday, couldn't get out, flooded either end of the village. Taunton was flooded too. Lost a day's pay. The first time Taunton flooded like this I was working in Moore's Corner House Cake shop where the Wimpy Bar is now right by the river. I worked up to my knees in water trying to save stuff. The sandbags are still there. I was born in Taunton. My mother worked on the railways as a cleaner, Great Western, during the war. She was a carriage cleaner. She worked all hours. Before the war it was a man's job, but she carried on after the war. My auntie and grandmother worked on munitions at Puriton. It was pretty dangerous. They were taken there to work every day. My mum worked all her life.

I got four brothers. My grandmother brought me up. I married at seventeen. First child eighteen. Married a man twenty-five years older than me. He had nine children out of eleven with him. Youngest four. You didn't expect that did you? His wife died. Then two of my

67

own. The marriage lasted nineteen years. I got a super husband now. We've been together twenty-three years. I started out as Brice, a grain of rice, then I became Mrs Yard. Now I am Fouracre. I've literally grown in size as well.

Last year we won the Loo of the Year Competition. Area category winner South West. They just turn up to judge. One of them's a man. But the ladies don't mind when it's explained to them. We have men coming in here with disabled wives and vice versa in the men's toilets. I could tell you lots of stories. You got to be careful. Some tongue in cheek, others not tongue in cheek... I get here 7.45am, finish at 6.30pm. I shut the door at six to give me time to clean up. At Christmas time it's all sort of jovial but it could get out of hand.

The walls are decorated with birds, ladybirds, dragonflies, butterflies. We got gnomes in here, cats, birds. The council even allowed me to choose the paint. Yellow. It was grey before. A lot of the Christmas stuff has been brought for me by other people. I've only been like this five years, when the full-time lady left. I asked the council if I could.

You've got to have a sense of humour. I don't think I can put any more up out there. Perhaps I have over gilded the lily... I get a lot of joy cleaning the sinks and seeing the taps gleam, the mirrors and the tiles. Most weeks I do around the flowers, they're all silk, no plastic ones or real ones. I like things matching. I pay for all this myself. I use bleach, disinfectant, cream cleaner and polish for the oak doors. I can remember them when I was a child. There was a turnstile. In one door and out the other.

World War Three would break out if they closed us down. It's a safety measure. And in this little room women can breast-feed their babies, leave their shopping, have a cup of tea or coffee. One old lady had her purse lifted, she hadn't even got the bus fair home to Burnham. I've had ladies been taken ill whilst pregnant. Instinct takes over then.

I retire when I am sixty-five. I have seven grandchildren of my own and two great-grandchildren. Then with the first lot, let's see. Francine had two, Judy had four, Leonora had two, Jacky had three, Maureen had three, Leonard had three, Vivien had three. There's more than that. Valerie - she's dead - she had two, Diane had two and Pat had four. How many's that? Twenty-eight, that's just the step-grandchildren. I see them all.

People come from Australia and New Zealand, specially sent to see me. There's a picture of this loo in a shopping mall in Australia. Internationally renowned we are. I get husbands dragged in just to see the flowers. We have nice soft toilet roll here and hot water. I get great joy. I enjoy my job. Humble as it is, I love my work. I get great joy. I've met a lot of people.

'Gone to seed'
Nancy Walker - Vegetable Seller, Muchelney

I was born here and was kicked in at the deep end, aged six, when my
brother went to war. He stood over my father and made him sign the
papers saying he was seventeen, when in fact he was only sixteen.

They sent him to Gibraltar for three years to live on the Rock with
the monkeys. So I had to help with all the farm work, getting the cows
in, milking, seeing to the young calves, hoeing mangolds, thinning
them out, then picking them, cutting them in halves and quarters
before putting them through the mill which was worked by hand. We
kept the farm going. Mother never liked cows, she was frightened of
them and Father never had a tractor. He worked with horses until 1962.
We never had a milking machine either and the electric only came in
1948. We used to take the milk up to the factory in Thorney by horse
and cart and sometimes deliver it round the village. In the floods some
would bring it up from Horsey Farm by boat.

We used to do embroidery round the lamp on the kitchen table, it
was a wonder we didn't lose our eyesight. Others of course did gloving.
There wasn't a lot else apart from cleaning. I used to help my friends
cut out the gloves on the frames they had. Course everyone had gloves
in those days. You never went to church without gloves. White in
summer, leather in winter. Mains water went through the village in
1912, but the Squire would not have it in any houses (he owned the
whole of Muchelney) and it was not until 1919 when circumstances
made him start selling the whole village that the owners had access to
mains water. We still have our well, in working order, on the front

lawn. I went to school across the road. No time lost in travelling. The teacher coped very well. We were about thirty kids and the same number again with evacuees, but I don't remember there being any trouble. As soon as I left school I got a job in Lloyds Bank in Langport. I met my husband there and then went away when I was twenty-one and lived in Midsomer Norton in the coal-mining area next to Norton Hill. I came back nineteen years later in 1973. That was when we got our first television.

After we gave up the milking herd we kept fat stock. My son was keen on market gardening and learnt from Bob Gooden at West Lambrook and then went to college. He started the vegetables in about 1983 as well as Pick Your Own. Raspberries didn't do so well, they went yellow, but strawberries, blackcurrants, loganberries and blackberries do well. We found all sorts of things on the farm, even a Roman coin, had it dated last year when I went on an archaeology course at Dillington. 330-333AD Emperor Constantine it was.

I am true Muchelney. There's others been here longer perhaps but we have been in the same house since my grandfather's time. I used to sell vegetables in the passageway, it was very cool there on the flagstones and you got a good breeze if both doors were open. My son lives there now and I am in the old stable.

Gone to seed... That's a bee bole behind me in the wall where they used to keep the bees in winter in a small skep and there's a pump trough, a North Devon pig salter, one of Serena de la Hey's willow geese, some of Mark Melbourne's pots and some of our flowers. I paint cards now which sell well. The cat's called Stumpy because he came to us with no tail.

'The dogs are therapy - Henry has attitude'
Caroline Jackson - Hospice Community Nurse, Nether Stowey

I was born in London in 1956, raised in Lincolnshire near the Fens. My father was a doctor and my mother was a nurse. So it was almost following in the family's footsteps. I only ever wanted to nurse. There was a picture of me dressed up in a nurse's uniform aged two on my father's desk. Interestingly enough his father was from farming stock in Worcestershire near Stourport. Mother's father was a coal miner in Northumberland. She was very proud of that.

I did my training at Addenbrookes in Cambridge. No desire to do medicine. Three years. Stayed on for six months and then went to London, just doing general medicine in hospitals. During that time I felt that, how shall I put it, when people are very ill and dying, they tended to be pushed to the end of the ward. I felt that there had to be more to the end of life and from that stemmed my interest in cancer nursing. I then went to the Royal Marsden to do their Oncology course and worked on a terminal care ward and came out with my Oncology certificate. All sorts of cancer, young and old. Just after I finished that, I bucked the system, decided I had had enough, put an advert in *The Lady* magazine and worked for a family in Suffolk. Three small children, a house cow, goats and pigs. Learned to milk the goats on the first night and the cow on the second - into buckets. Nanny, farmworker and general factotum. Huge fun. Completely different, fairly off-beat, an education. Three months, then went off to Australia with a friend I had met at the Marsden. I nursed in Melbourne at the Freemasons' hospital and then did Australia by Greyhound bus.

Sydney, Adelaide, Ayer's Rock, Queensland, Cairns, the Barrier Reef. Back to Sydney, then to Perth. Ran out of money in Perth, did emergency housekeeping for various families then got the train back to Sydney. Christmas with an uncle in the Hunter Valley then six weeks in New Zealand. I decided I didn't want to come back nursing, so I stayed eighteen months with the same family in Suffolk. My leaving present was a front door key... I applied back to Addenbrookes. They expected their nurses to go off and then come back. I met one of the senior nurses who said 'why aren't you up on the Oncology ward?' I was senior staff nurse for fourteen months at which point I wanted a Sister's post. Cambridge being Cambridge, no one leaves. So I did my midwifery - Mum always said it would come in handy, and I ended up in Taunton in 1985. Eighteen months there and at Yeovil. Midwifery was not for me. The saving grace was the community midwife at Martock. She was marvellous. I was a challenge!

My tutor told me about the embryonic St Margaret's Hospice. I made inquiries and got a Junior Sister's job before it ever opened. That was April 1987. Three-quarters of it is funded by charity. People are brilliant. It combined Oncology, general experience, terminal care, a natural progression. All my previous experience. In the In-Patient Unit we offered palliative care, all people with uncurable diseases. Mainly cancer. I was there for six years. Sixteen beds.

Then I've been out in the community six years. People are referred to me from their GP's surgery, hospital or hospice. It is supporting patients and their families in their homes, a supportive and advisory role. No hands-on nursing, I nursed my own mother ten years ago and I came back a different person. More sympathetic, more realistic, more

empathy. Families handle death differently. People don't know what's normal, or how to act. Our society is very bad at preparing people for it. Seeing people earlier in the diagnosis is better. We are very much a secondary service. Personally I have a strong Christian faith, but there is often a lot of anger about. People feel cheated. You can't be sanctimonious. Nowadays sixty is young to die. You try to help people to accept. People never cease to amaze me. Some accept this is what's happening, they just accept it. If they are in pain, letting go can be a relief. We try to make them as comfortable as possible. Some people talk of an after-life. A lot of people say that's it. You really get to know people. You almost become part of their families. In many ways it can be a real privilege.

It is up to me how I arrange my caseload. Sometimes you build up a relationship like old friends. Ideally you don't take on the grief but occasionally you get close. I help people to recognise what is normal. Grief sometimes catches you out unawares, much, much later. They can always contact me at work any time.

My therapy is walking the dogs. Tosca is nine. Five or six years ago I started with a friend, gun dog classes on Exmoor near Dunster. I used to go picking up near Wellington, but now I just do beating. The dogs stay at home in the summer but come with me in the car during the winter. Periodically they come in to see the patients. Patients say 'are you married?' 'No.' 'Have you got children?' 'No ... Well, I do have two, they're black and they've got four legs each.' Henry has attitude. He's a real beater's dog but he needs a firm hand. They love it, they'll retrieve anything. I love being outside, I love the elements, the people I meet, real Somerset people and the fact that nobody's really interested in your working life. I take a great pride in my dogs.

Two years ago I had a sabbatical. Six months off work, nine weeks in Kenya with three different hospices; the conditions - a real eye opener. A month in Nairobi, lived with an African family. I worked in the Out-Patients clinic. Things that we take for granted; they ran out of bottles for medicine, and tape. Huge, huge amount of AIDS. I think the biggest culture shock was in Nairobi Hospital. Two to a bed, mattresses on the floor, no mosquito nets, quite a lot of families helped with the nursing.

Death does get to me at times. I see easily sixty, seventy people a year. I'd like to do something slightly different. I need to be with well people some of the time. I need my life outside. It's an easy job to get sucked into. Often I've got nothing left to give emotionally. That's me. The long-term effect. The dogs are therapy. They are always raring to go. Being in Somerset is almost like coming home, there are real parallels with the Fens.

There are seven stages to grief. Sadness, anger, loss, loneliness, guilt, letting go... relief. It hits people in different ways at different times. Families vary. I usually go twice after a death, if it's wanted, but they always have my work number. Some don't want to see me, it's a reminder. Others phone me up months afterwards. The more rural the family the better they are at accepting it.

I love life, I really do. I only want to do it once. No rehearsals. One thing about this job it makes me take one day at a time. I really live each day. As for death you can't always tell when it's going to happen. There is a point when they let go. Dad died this summer, the beginning of June. Chest infection.

'Women make very good masons'
Evelyn Body - Sculptor, Thorney Mill

I was born at Windsor. My father was an Army officer and we all left on a troopship to Malaya when I was thirteen months old. On board I nearly died. Diarrhoea and vomiting, some ghastly bug went round the ship and I was kept alive with a pipette made from a fountain pen. I also learnt to swim before I could walk. The journey took two months because the Suez Canal was shut. We went to Kuala Lumpur and lived in the jungle. It was frightening then... a Communist uprising, guerrilla warfare. My mother found a beautiful teapot abandoned in the jungle at the bottom of the garden, she still has tea out of it today. We had Chinese servants and I spent most of my time with them round the back of the house. I have always loved Chinese people since then. I remember sitting in the dust under a table while they ate. I loved the smell. It was just the best part of my life. I remember sitting on a beach with my mother, watching the fishermen pulling their nets in and I can remember their song exactly.

I was four or five when I left and came back to England. Always we were moving. Germany was horrible. Five to six years. Always moving every eighteen months. There is so much travelling in my life. My father was with his regiment. His father was also an Army officer. My mother's father was a stockbroker and his father was a bookie. We have always liked the horses in our family and on my mother's side was Frederick Treves, a doctor who did the first appendix operation and looked after the Elephant Man...

I went to Army schools. Really grim, I was bullied incessantly as my father was commanding the regiment. At eleven I was sent to a boarding school in Salisbury. My parents lived in Thailand for four years and then in Greece. My father was military attaché at the embassy. Both of these countries are important for sculpture. Thailand for the enormous reclining Buddhas, and in Greece the National Archaeological Museum. That is where I fell in love with sculpture. Then I went to Bournemouth Art College, specialising in sculpture and drawing after a foundation course. Then I wanted to carve stone. Nobody knew how to cut it at the college so I went to Weymouth Tech, stonemasonry and carving, and started to earn my living. I lived at Wolfeton House, a medieval gatehouse which we managed to partly burn down. I was away... We re-built it. I got married to an Army officer on St Aldhem's Head who then left the Army and became a joiner. My granny died and left me enough money to buy a house at Lopen. I just carried on making sculpture. All commissions. I worked in stone, clay and plaster and drew. Mainly Portland stone.

My first stonemasonry job was for Dorset County Council. 'We have got a mural we would like you to make in a school at Southwell'. I was to work in the Bath & Portland Stone sheds, with stone supplied by Easton Masonry. That cocktail, given to a woman, an outsider, on Portland... when I think about it now... I was only twenty... a Molotov cocktail... Easton Masonry kept supplying shelly stone, and I kept sending it back. The same Geoff Smith who had the trouble with French stone at the British Museum... It wasn't easy. It has always been really difficult for me, because I have chosen to work in a profession that is male-dominated... Actually stone is so heavy that most is lifted by machine. Women make very good masons... they have very steady qualities that makes them good masons, and they have the light touch you need for carving, a delicate touch... Men can have a very old-fashioned view of women, particularly in traditional industries like the quarrying of stone... What I have now learnt is that I can go into a male-dominated workplace, be completely myself and still be accepted.

Commissions are great and exciting and I fight to get them. Once I have got them they are very hard work because I am a single parent with two children and a large rotting house that gets flooded for a pastime. I have done a big job for Sainsbury's in Street, a bronze for the Riverside in Taunton, Timestones on Ham Hill, three life-size figures of Apollo, Dionysus and Diana for a garden in Cirencester, and this relief carving for the Tacchi Morris Centre, also in Taunton.

I love my teaching. Textile and fashion students, life drawing at SCAT... and young kids. The ability to play is where creativity lies, and the source that I return to, is to observe what is out there and discover. Drawing is a great way to do that.

This is one of my three grandsons, Robert, he's fourth generation farming and the teddy is seventy years old. I've been here since 1960, so that's forty years. We had no electric then. The generator came in 1968 and we've been like that ever since. No mains at all, even now. We only have it on at night when we need it, but it's not really a problem. It starts automatically but if you switch your light off, and it doesn't stop, it means there's one light on somewhere and you've got to hunt for it. I've got a freezer now but it's well trained. We never had a fridge of course and used to keep the milk cool in churns with water from a well at the back of the house. We miss milking but we could never have coped with the bulk tankers.

I just accept things, that's how I am. I used to wash the clothes in the boiler, that was hard work but my mother-in-law used to do it. Then I had a twin tub till 1979. Farming is a way of life. Joe, that's my husband, his mother would have been 100 today if she'd have lived, she was very Victorian. Washed on Monday, ironed on Tuesday, bedrooms on Wednesdays... Sometimes I feel guilty if I sit down. But then I didn't drive till 1967, I always used the bicycle, but people delivered in those days. Bread three times a week. If I wanted to go to Yeovil I would cycle to Haselbury and get the bus and just hope you didn't get a puncture on the way back. Pace of life was different then. You get used to working all hours. Time doesn't matter so much. You get used to doing the meals. They always want their food on time. There's no lying in bed on a farm. You've got to work together. I help with the

sheep. But then I did take a part-time job at Lawrence's in the Fine Art department and helped with the viewing. My daughter worked there. That was good, to get out every so often, and mix with other people.

When I first started work it was at the sail cloth firm in Crewkerne, Richard Hayward in the office. They made webbing at that time. That was before I got married, I worked there eight years and would come in from West Chinnock where I was born... We'd find it strange to have neighbours now. The nearest farm is half a mile away. When we enter our lane we know we are home. The gypsies used to live in the lane but that was a few years ago. They brought the Queen of the Gypsies back here when she died, and cremated her in her gypsy wagon.

My husband and son-in-law help run the South Somerset Preservation Club and help organise Yesterday's Farming. Husband is President and son-in-law is Chairman, so it's in the family... We never had a holiday. Joe never got wages. We give George a wage, but we take out his keep. This is a family farm and we own it. One hundred and sixty acres. We do our own meat and keep the freezer full. No BSE. We've got poultry and our own vegetables. No electric cooker of course but I do have a Rayburn, runs on wood and coal. An oil-fired one would be nice but everything outside always comes first. Housewife's needs come last. I even do all the decorating. I am one for family life and fortunate in having a good family. The money is all ploughed back into the farm. It used to be Joe and his brother. Granddad always kept the chequebook and then we bought Joe's brother out and now it's Samways and Son. Wages, you must be joking.

Pleasure always comes last. We are ourselves and we don't have to keep up with the Joneses. In April we topped the market in Yeovil and Taunton with our Charolais steers. When we started the sheep, they were cheaper than children's toys. We've always had about 200. I spin some of the wool up from the sheep in jumpers for the grandchildren.

Last year was the first year we didn't make cider. Joe had his hip done. We always picked up apples in the autumn half term, when the kids were around and we always paid people in cider, if they helped us out on the farm with odd jobs during the year. But you can't get anybody now, they're all off earning more in offices and factories. But now we are on the pension we've never been so well off... I still make my own pastry. You just get on with it and bake when I feel like it. Farming was better then... not the paperwork. Pace of life was different... You don't want that rat race. We've got good friends in East Coker and when people are ill, everyone rallies round. Farming... you've got to work together. I just accepted things... that's how I am.

'It was a labour of love'
Margaret Spencer - Rocking Horse Specialist, Crewkerne

I was born in Lancashire and brought up in Hampshire. My father was an Electrical Engineer but he was very much a DIY man. He taught me how to use tools and my mother taught me how to make patterns. Her family were in the cotton industry. Both my grandmothers had their own businesses. One lived at the bottom of the Pennines selling lemonade to walkers and fresh eggs. All that marvellous country. Grandfather didn't like going to church so he'd say to my mother 'hey kid, let's go for a trounce'. He was a spinner in the cotton mills and Grandmother was a weaver but he lost his job because he lost the use of his hands. Mother went to the department stores when they had sales and bought up what wasn't sold and then sold it on the poor at so much a week. Only they didn't get the clothes till they'd finished paying for it. She kept a book but some of them had no name, so she just wrote in sayings like 'Anything Fresh' or 'I won't come in, I've got my clogs on'. My other grandmother helped run a bowling green. Nobody was allowed to swear, she was 4ft and would send them off the green by the scruff of the neck, kneeing them in the small of the back. Grandfather made the crowned greens.

We moved around a lot in the Thirties. I was always messing about in Father's garage. I used to whittle. During the war I had made a battleship about eighteen inches long, matchsticks for guns. I never finished it, because that was boys' work... I worked in my father's shop for a while and then worked in Winchester. I got married to my childhood sweetheart. We knew each other since we were thirteen.

We came to Crewkerne in 1951. I became a tracer, tracing maps for the electricity board to give to engineers when they went out on a job. I did that till '56. I had three children and was also a Dinner Lady at school. When the youngest daughter was due to go to school I wanted something in the home that paid. My mother was an Antique Dealer. My father bought an old rocking horse and took it apart to see how it was made. He started to make one. In the Sixties there was a lack of good toys. It was sold before he had finished it. He then encouraged me. 'Here's a load of wood, go home and make one,' he said. And if my dad said I could make one, I could. It took me six months. I'll show you if you like. I used to do it in the passageway. Pinched my husband's tools of course. He was an Electrical Engineer as well. I had no plans. Since then I have made 500 rocking horses in about thirty years. All orders. No room to show them. In the summer I would carve out the heads, block up the bodies and cut out the legs... Nearly all dapple greys. Everyone wanted a dapple grey. To start with, pine with beech legs. Latterly, mostly lime with beech legs. English lime. Close grain without being heavy. You can carve with the grain, against the grain and across the grain. Some of the pine came from demolition. Old beams. Nearly all the rest kiln-dried from timber merchants.

I used to have horses and bits of horse all along the hallway and stacked up on the landing. I used to leave them for at least a fortnight before finishing so the wood could move. It would take about forty hours to make a small horse, fifty hours a medium and sixty a large one. I also had one person doing restorations. Only two ever came back. Some had been through five boys. Horses on rockers were called Toe Crunchers and swingers Shin Bashers. The first horse I sold for

£25. The last one for £1,000. All signed and numbered on the actual horse. Plates can be removed or put on.

I could never get on with the spokeshave, surform were better, round ones, curved ones and then mechanical sanders. Recently I have used a lot more power tools. Mallets and chisels. The main chisel I used is now half the length it used to be due to sharpening. I always make each horse's head differently, different ears and nostrils. I even designed a push-me-pull-me horse with two heads and two children sit on it back to back. And then there is all the tack and child-friendly paint. My horses have gone all over the world. New Zealand, Australia, Saudi, Israel, Canada, USA, France, Belgium, Germany – that was the birthplace of rocking horses before Charles the First's time. Even the Army used them for recruits before the Second World War, to teach them to stay in the saddle, only they have half-round rockers which are much deeper than the normal oval rockers. It used to be a punishment to sit there for an hour... The manes are all horsehair.

If something is worth doing it's worth doing well. No short cuts. It was a labour of love. I'm now writing my second book...

'Doors open at twelve'
Nancy Berrey - Volunteer, Montacute House

I was born in 1922 in British North Borneo - Kinabalu. My father was a
District Officer. No school. I left with my sister when I was seven.
Father stayed on another four years. Hill country. Tenom. Dayaks -
head-hunters. We had a pet baby orang-utan, a darling monkey called
Martha, she had to have her own toothbrush and learnt to use the
thunder box. Lots of snakes, all poisonous except for the python which
would squeeze you to death. I dislike snakes to this day and I still tip
up shoes to get rid of scorpions. When the Japanese came not many of
the British women survived the camps.

Father joined Cable and Wireless and was sent to St Helena. During
the First World War he was a pilot and flew Sopwith Camels for the
Fleet Air Arm. He crashed and injured his back and leg. He married
my mother in 1918 and simply said 'pack up your bags, we are going
to Borneo'. My sister was nine months old. My mother's family had
been doctors in Olney for 500 years. I was supposed to be a doctor but I
wasn't good enough at Latin.

We had a very lovely childhood. Excellent education, marvellous
holidays on the Ouse. Played with a gang of boys swimming all over
the place. Whole lot got killed in the war except for one.

Started nursing at Alton. All outdoor nursing, TB etc, didn't like it. Got
terrible earache. 'Show no hair Nurse,' the matron used to say. Then ARP
duty in Olney, Father was in the Observer Corps at Newport Pagnell. I
volunteered for the Wrens in 1940 and was called up in 1941. Went to
Westfield College in Hampstead and did a course for six

months in Chelsea Polytechnic on electrics and radio, then went to a Naval Air Station in Scotland and learnt how to fit and service radar in Swordfish and Albacores. Unofficially, I also flew testing the sets.

Then up to Donibristle in Fife, and over to Machrihanish - the Mull of Kintyre. We took over from the men who then had to go to sea. The planes went to carriers off the Clyde. One carrier was sunk with all hands just after the planes were flown on. But that was hushed up. I was a leading Wren and then a Petty Officer.

I was commissioned at Greenwich. Three weeks' training, and sent to HMS *Ariel*. Radio as well as radar. I had to take divisions with 1,000 men. A Sergeant of Marines taught me how to give commands and make your voice carry. Radios were primitive. Almost the cat's whisker. I supervised the repairs.

Then I was sent back to Fife to Crail where they opened a new grass aerodrome for aircraft that had been repaired. I was there till 1944. They then wanted to sent me to a remote airfield in Australia but they worked out I would have been the only woman for 500 miles so they thought better of it... I went to a Naval Air Station just outside Cape Town in the *bundu*. The mimosa was wonderful. I was in charge of sixty men and had a request from the Chief Petty Officer that they should not be called 'Nancy Boys'... I returned by troop train to Durban at 25mph. I was wearing 'whites' that became black by the end.

Then on a troop ship back home. A week in Mombasa. We had the first evacuated Japanese Prisoners of War on board. Skeletons. Every day one or two more thrown over the side.

In 1948 I got married to a Lieutenant Commander who then became a very senior Captain. Supply Branch. Admiral's Secretary. Once worked for Mountbatten. Marvellous brain but not easy to work for.

Lived next to Richmond Park, then in Hamburg. Stayed in Goering's House on the Elbe. He had an 11ft bed. All the paintings had disappeared but the curtains and carpets were in place. Things were so bad in Germany that they would take out tea from the teapot, dry it and use it again. Hamburg had been hammered but they cleared up very quickly and put it down to grass, much better than London was.

We came to South Petherton in 1957. I took a job in Yeovil as a librarian. And then worked as an overseer for Meals on Wheels for Yeovil Rural District. Nine rounds, twice a week. I did that for twelve years. And was churchwarden for four years.

Then in 1984 I was taken on as a volunteer at Montacute House. Younger children love it. I did three days a week, now only one. Doors open at twelve. My favourite room is the Crimson Room. It has a good feeling about it. The big bed was made for James I. Each portrait fascinates me. History... I hear the most ghastly things being said. The public can often be a problem. Mobiles not allowed and as for men wearing baseball hats on back to front...

'I still feel ever-so young'
Doris Pile - Matron and Bellringer, Crewkerne

I was born at Bluntsmoor Farm between Misterton and Mosterton.
That was 1917. Father owned the farm. It was about 100 acres. We had
cows, pigs and chickens. We had to milk when we came back from
Mosterton School. Three cows each. If it was raining father would pick
us up with a pony and trap. We used to like that. Mother made butter
and cheese. She came from Burstock near Broadwindsor. My other
grandfather lived at Midnell Farm near Winsham. Father was very
fond of cider, but he contracted pneumonia when I was seven and died
three days later. There were no drugs then. The oxygen came from
Exeter by train. He smoked a lot... we had a wonderful cigarette
album. He was forty-three. We left the farm. It had to be sold. One
hundred acres, house, and two cottages. £6,000. All we could get. We
then moved in with my grandparents at Drimpton just by the bridge.
A wonderful man my grandfather. Sometimes the river flooded.

Mother was very keen on education. My brother went to Beaminster
Grammar School. My sister went to a boarding school at Burnham
and I went to the London Orphan School in Watford. There were lots of
fatherless children after the First War. Mother had to petition several
people to get me in. Children from academic families were top of the
list and farmers' children were at the bottom. I've still got the school
photograph. The only time we met with the boys was in chapel or at
meals, but there was no question of talking. I've still got two friends
from there. One in Canada, the other in Topsham. Food? Supper was
dried bread. Bread and dripping, that was good, and cake on Sundays.

I couldn't stand porridge or butter beans. At half term we were allowed visitors. But of course Mother couldn't make it. My sister had a thin time of it as well. I never liked school much. After boarding school you weren't fussy at all.

I stayed there till I was fifteen. Then did nursery training in Bristol, then nurse training at Bristol General next to the docks, and then did midwifery at Southmead. We had to pay to go to preliminary training. Mother had to find that. Then we got £12 a year in the first year, £15 in the second and £20 in the third. We were all in the same boat. I remember Neville Chamberlain declaring war on the radio. We listened to it in one of the nurse's rooms. One girl burst into tears she had two or three brothers. The first planes I saw were very high, about forty. Half an hour later we heard that Filton had been bombed. We used to go for egg, chips, bread and butter in Jones's for 1s/2d till it got bombed. At the General we had a land mine and a burst water main. We had to evacuate the whole hospital at night during the raid. Half of them went to the Infirmary and the others went to Weston. We used to shelter underground but we could hear the horses' hooves on the cobbles above us, so it can't have been that thick. Down in the shelter you would come across lots of bodies that had been brought in. On night duty I used to hang out over the rail and watch the boats come up into Bathurst Basin.

Then I went back to the Infirmary, the BRI where I was Junior Night Sister and then Senior Night Sister. We used to check on all patients three times a night, just to check that they were still breathing. Forty-one patients to each ward. What I wanted was a men's surgical ward. And I stayed there twenty years. In those days only men were doctors and only women were nurses. No women doctors. No male nurses. When men did start coming in it was very difficult but we got used to it. It was tough going, you'd have to do their work for them...

I came to Crewkerne in 1965. Mother was failing. There was a job going in Theatre and Out-Patients. Very nice, very pleasant, gorgeous. I knew a lot of people. Only twenty-eight beds... Appendix, hernias, simple mastectomies. I was Matron there for twelve years and retired when I was sixty. Then I put my feet on the mantelpiece. One day I was responsible for everything and then next day nothing. It is a most extraordinary feeling.

Now I do bellringing Monday nights. It's fun. I still ring the treble bell. They say I am very steady. Crewkerne has a fine set of bells, some of the best in the country. I also still play golf up at Windwhistle. My handicap used to be seventeen, now it is thirty-four. I still do eighteen holes. Marvellous views down to Charmouth and out to Steep Holm in the Bristol Channel. I visit friends who are ill. I still feel ever-so young when I pick people up in my car.

'From horticulture to dog collar'
Elfrida Savigear - Rector, Bicknoller

I came to Somerset in 1980 to be Head of Science at Cannington
Agricultural College. I was there ten years and taught Soil Science,
Plant Science, Pests and Diseases to horticultural students. My
original degree was from Wye College, a BSc Hons. I did an Adult
Education course at Edinburgh and then taught for seven years at
Merrist Wood College near Guildford. I have an MSc from Bath in
Plant Viruses and Tissue Culture and studied the problems of Lettuce
Big Vein in commercial growing - that was in 1984.

At the colleges I worked with full-time students but also took one-
day courses in pesticides and pesticide application. I was the first
woman to get the NPTC certification. I used to teach the use of
knapsack sprayers, glasshouse sprayers and fumigation. Both theory
and practical. On courses I would try to get them to use the right doses
and wear correct protective clothing. I also ran day conferences on
organic farming. Of course some of the organic sprays are fairly nasty.
Few of the organic chemicals have gone through the normal controls
and a little knowledge is a dangerous thing. In the end they're all
chemicals anyway. We forget that DDT also saved a lot of lives.

In 1990 I was looking ahead at where my life was going. If I stayed
on in the world of agricultural colleges, I would have had to move to
become a Vice-Principal somewhere, but that would have been more
administrative. So I went forward into the unknown. Four years
without pay at Theological College, just seeing what doors opened. I
did one year at Trinity College in Bristol. At this stage I did not know

whether I would even be ordained Priest. The main decision was taken by Synod on 11th November 1992. By that time I was at Cambridge, at Ridley College for two years. We would have become Deacons. I also did a thesis on Implicit Religion and Natural Belief Systems. It was a Lambeth Diploma. The main training had little emphasis on the problems in rural parishes. It was mostly essay writing. I was ordained Deacon in June 1993 in Hereford Cathedral and a year later as Priest. This was six weeks after the first ordination of women in the diocese, so we were the second batch. Four men and four women. It was very special and all my friends and supporters came. I did my curacy in Ross-on-Wye. I was there four years and the team looked after six villages. I then went to Warwickshire for twenty months. I had hoped to come to Somerset earlier.

This vacancy appeared two summers ago with interviews in autumn 1998. I came here in January '99. I look after six parishes called The Quantock Towers Benefice with seven churches - Bicknoller, Crowcombe, Monksilver, Elworthy, Nettlecombe, Sampford Brett and Stogumber. There is usually a service in each church every Sunday. I have three Readers and one Assistant Priest to help me. On Sundays I take four services, 8am, 9.30am, 11am and 6.30pm. I work Mondays so that I can process all the information I have gathered on Sunday. I enjoy putting people in touch with each other as I cover such a wide area. I take Tuesdays off and usually go swimming in Watchet. Yesterday I bought a sheepdog puppy, eight weeks old from a farm at Clatworthy. I have a sheepdog called Zyppa who sometimes comes into church and Pixie, my mum's sheltie, who is thirteen.

Then there are endless meetings. Lots of Parochial Church Council meetings. I am a governor at two schools, Crowcombe and Stogumber, and I love the children. Then there are weddings, baptisms and funerals. We had thirty-eight funerals last year. Five in May when I was away. At All Saints' Day we have a special service for all the bereaved families - elsewhere on that day I had a toddler service in another village and a communion service in a third. One of the things I have done is got a list of all the farmers and we are trying to get them to put down on paper their horror stories of how bad farming really is and then it will be sent to the Diocesan Synod. Depression is commonplace. Three dairy herds have gone in eighteen months and another is going.

The main comment I had from parishioners was that they could hear me, which was their way of saying that they thought I was all right. I can stay here till I am seventy unless I do something dreadful. Every morning I go up walking on the Quantocks.

I can honestly say, God is very busy in all the parishes.

I am a local person. I was born at East Lambrook. My mother came
from East Lambrook and my father from Lower Burrow. My mum's
dad was a stonemason. He used to do churches and cathedral work,
Fry's of Kingsbury. My father done all sorts, the last job was at
Yandles' wood yard at Martock. He worked the crane, a very big crane
it's still there. My neighbour drives it now, they used to do a lot of
coffins. Before that he used to work on a bakery round, Legg's of
Kingsbury, before that he was in the Army and before that he was on
the farm. His father was a farmer, he did withies, a small-holding. My
grandmother, she did gloving all her life, sat in the window, she never
left Lower Burrow hardly ever. Everybody used to visit. 'Do bring
milk,' she used to say, 'otherwise you can't have a cup of tea.' She
always done leather prixseam, which is very technical. She had the
machine in her home, treadle not electric, treadles went out in the late
1950s. She was gloving right up to the day she died.

'I am going to sit down and have a rest,' she used to say when she
worked. They used to work all hours right up till Saturday midnight,
but not on Sunday. Church on Sunday. My aunt is 100 and she started
gloving when she was nine so if she was born in 1900 that means she
started work in 1909.

Even when I left school most of us went into the glove factory. You
couldn't get out of the village easily. I was fifteen when I came here,
that's Reed's. By that time I had moved to Kingsbury. There were
forty, forty-five working here then. Now it is twenty, twenty-one. And

out-workers there must have been about sixty, it took one person all week to sort out the work and deliver it. Out on one Wednesday and then back on the next. Kingsbury, Langport, Long Sutton, South Petherton, Ilminster, even Yeovil.

There's about thirteen out-workers now. The firm of Reeds was started by Millicent Reed. Miss Reed's mother was a Bag Woman. She co-ordinated the outwork and would connect with the train at Thorney. She set up her own green shed and then expanded. The firm is now owned by Southcombe's of Stoke-sub-Hambdon. They have still got the work's hooter in Stoke and sometimes we can hear it over here.

There are no short cuts with the gloves. It is quite a skill. We used to get paid £3/10/9 for a forty-two hour week, eight till six, five on Fridays and one hour for lunch. We now take an hour for lunch and get Friday afternoons off. Some was time-work, some was piece-work. We used to get paid 3s 6d a dozen. Nylon simplex. Ladies wore dress gloves, particularly at Easter, all sorts of colours. We have new machines from Japan, but they are not that much different. Same basics. The glove is already cut out to the shape of the hand. There is the trank, the fitting and then the thumb. It's a bit awkward to describe the glove.

I've never been short of work. Mostly women's gloves, but then there's men's white ceremonial marching gloves for the MoD, all fabric. The ladies' dress fashion gloves have all gone, but we do ladies' and men's thermal gloves. At Southcombe's they do outdoor activity gloves and used to do police motorbike gloves, but we don't do any leather here. Then there's football gloves for supporters. They are rushed off their feet at the moment, they got their seasons mixed up.

1963 I think I came here. You get your ups and downs, usually we have the radio on. The girls like to listen to music, personal stereos. I like Orchard FM. Sometimes one of the girls sings. It helps the day on. I usually make sixty to seventy pairs a day. Some of the girls are much quicker. Every pair is 100 percent examined. They don't miss very much. I like putting the thumbs in, just stitch round. I've done pointing, elasticating, blind-topping, needle-topping, welting, rucking, strap-fitting. Some customers have joint-fitting which in Devon is called 'nicketts'. Then there's ironing. An iron like a hand that you pull the glove over, a brass-heated hand. You have to have the temperature low for thermal gloves otherwise they melt... You sit long enough. I did work at home when I had children which was convenient, or if your children were off school and ill you simply took the head off your machine and took it home. I walk to work. Mum always done gloving and my husband is a Bricklayer. We're the only glove factory that does everything from beginning to end.

'People just love to hear about our orchard'
June Small - Apple Grower, Creech St Michael

I'm just me... I was born in Brighton. Most of my young life was spent in High Wycombe. My mother's family were in the furniture business. My father's family were in the theatre. Grandmother used to sing, a music hall star, and then played the piano for the silent films in London. My father was an engineer and a very good artist. School... and then I went to teacher training college and then taught primary in an RAF school, Medmenham outside Marlow. Wonderful school. Kids far better travelled than I was. Two years there, and then Robin came out of the Navy and decided to go fruit-growing.

We came down to Taunton in 1958 and fell in love with the place. We found two fruit orchards, which each required a person. One of the owners was chairman of the school in Creech. We fell on our feet. After two years the farmer here sold the orchard and Robin with it. No fruit training but he did do a course when he was leaving the Navy. He had thought of making the Navy his career but then he met me...

After three years Robin was made a partner and it grew from four to forty-four acres. Gradual planting on fields that had wheat. This was the farm. By that time I had two children. I was still at Creech St Michael School and was head of the infant department, 1970 to '80. So I had two jobs. In the orchard, I was delivering and packing, but never allowed to do the pruning. It was a man's job... And then about that time I joined the Somerset Women's Farmer's Union. I was a founder member. We were very forward-thinking. I was secretary.

My first public office. The promotion of farm products became a focus. Quite vociferous... visited the supermarkets and complained... Took farmers into supermarkets, showed them their products and what the public expected. We did promote farming very strongly - Taste of Somerset, which then evolved into Taste of the West. We concentrated on local food, pointing out to the public that it made sense environmentally. Somerset eggs going up to Kent and Kent eggs coming down to Somerset was absurd. Supermarkets had no idea what goes on on farms.

It was amazing what women could do. We could get the top man in Sainsbury's in ten minutes. I remember meeting Sir Charles Forte and many other top people and discussing how our produce was displayed and marketed on their shelves. The NFU's little tractor is working.

In the meantime I took early retirement and the Women's Farm and Garden Association, originally Land Girls, was looking for someone to represent them on COPA, the Committee of Professional Agriculturalists. There are a lot more women's committees in Europe. We are very reticent in the UK. They get a lot of sponsorship. We have visited a lot of countries. It's voluntary. We don't get paid. I've been to Venice, Barcelona, Helsinki. Each time we go we meet farmers and their families.

Diversification is important - tourism on farms. You discover that everybody is in the same boat. In Finland I gave a paper on how we have diversified. We were way ahead. But still things are very slow moving. Equal pay, equal pension rights, divorce settlements... If you want a gripe I'll give you one. If I don't go to represent the UK at these COPA meetings the UK is sometimes not represented. I have taken it up with the Euro MP, the NFU, Parliament. I need sponsorship. If I don't go no one does. A very difficult situation... Because I am five foot, I often get overlooked by men in a group. So... I have to be a bit aggressive. I take a box with me. I was very quiet beforehand.

People just love to hear about our orchard, the jobs you have to do, the problems, the disease, pests ... What we have actually done is started to grow traditional well-flavoured apples. Then we set about educating the public's palate, talking to the public at shows and exhibitions, school and open days. It is also helped by Common Ground. James Ravilious took lots of pictures. We live down a No Through Road, we have to lure people with a lot of publicity. We do have to work hard. Taunton Farmers' Markets are very successful. We had to fight for that. Last Thursday of the month. We do seven others. Bridgwater is one of the best. Face-to-face with the public.

We have thirty-two different varieties of apple, fourteen different apple juices as well as quinces, plums, pumpkins and squashes. Jams, jellies and herbs. People come from all over the place. On Twelfth Night we wassail our trees to ensure a good crop.

'We can guarantee the hat but we can't guarantee the weather'
Pennie Hill - Ladies' Hat Hirer, Stoke-sub-Hamdon

I was born in Bridgwater. My father was in business there for a long
time. A wholesale grocer. He died quite young, when I was small, a
very good businessman. I remember huge vats of dark sugar, big jars
of sweets and large cheeses. He was very good to the local hospital at
Christmas and would send along the big crackers, old-fashioned
Christmas decorations and skipping ropes. His shop was in St Mary
Street and had a big crest above the door with the Bridgwater coat of
arms. It is now a nightclub.

He bought the mill in Blake Street opposite my grandfather's house.
It had been powered by an underground stream. He used it for storage.
Grandfather was an accountant for a local brewery. My father's health
was not good, he had TB and had to go and live in Switzerland, so I
spent quite a lot of my childhood there and so I learnt skiing at an
early age. My father died in about 1951.

On the other side of the family my mother was from Southern
Ireland and her father was a policeman in County Cork. It was during
the trouble in the Twenties and they were driven out, so they were
refugees and chose Taunton by sticking a pin in a map. There was also
a farming background there and the last of the land in County
Tipperary was sold quite recently. The markets there were amazing.
You could exchange secondhand shoes and park your car in the middle
of the street.

I went to school in Otterhampton. St Hilda's. Girls brought their
ponies and every girl could swim. I worked at Lloyds Bank in

Bridgwater and Taunton. In those days only one or two women worked as cashiers, but my grandfather always said 'one day it will be all girls as cashiers'. How right he was. I worked behind the scenes for four or five years. I was christened, confirmed and married in St Mary's Church.

My husband's family were all farmers and doctors on one side and vets and nurses on the other. They came from Devon. When we bought the farm forty years ago we had a large mortgage. The land is very good, soil like at South Petherton. We had 160 acres and the house and made do with all people's throw-outs for furniture. The lane was very rough. We grow mostly potatoes, Estima, Desiree and Cara. They go to Branston's and then to Tesco's mainly. The wet weather was awful. Last autumn was a real battle. They do work incredibly hard. It's crazy but it's interesting.

As to hats, I have been running Ahead for Hats for eight years. I have a partner, Ruth Chant from Martock. She was a farmer's daughter. The idea was born at a wedding. A very nice wedding, a friend's daughter (I often get asked to do the flowers). And after a few glasses of champagne the topic turned to hats. How difficult it was to get hats, how expensive they were, and there was a table with lots of hats on. I don't know how it happened, I was sitting next to Ruth and we just said that would be a lovely thing to do, to hire out hats, and we started on the Monday morning.

Everything else you can justify because you can wear them again. A pair of shoes, a suit, a coat, a nice dress. But there is real guilt involved with buying a hat for over £100. Even men understand it now, and they thank us for setting up. It saves them a small fortune.

We have hats made and choose the fabric. Several firms in London. We go round the millinery departments. We would not be in business if we were not up to standard. Officially, women hire the hats for the weekend, Friday till Monday, but some like to extend the weekend. They come back bubbling with excitement promising photographs, we get notes in the boxes and even wedding cake. One classic dress and a different hat each time. Very therapeutic. Gives ladies a lot of confidence.

Every year we buy in new stock. Each hat has a number, but like farmers getting to know their sheep we get to know each one individually. They get used for all sorts of occasions. Weddings, graduations, fundraisings, garden parties at the Palace, Henley, institutions, military events, the races. As we say we can guarantee the hat but we can't guarantee the weather. If it's raining we just advise ladies to find a man with a large umbrella and stick with him all afternoon.

Some people choose in ten minutes, others take ten hours. Some say that they are a non-hat person and we soon convert them, until they are out scouring the countryside looking for weddings to go to. We stock an exciting collection. The display room is the old dairy.

'A bit of a rebel'
Angie Allen - Painter and Decorator, South Petherton

I was born in Crewkerne. One of the few that drink in Oscar's wine bar
that was actually born there. We had pubs. We had The Admiral Hood
in Mosterton, but it was called The New Inn then. The pub burnt down
on November 5th, 1955. A sky rocket. A thatched roof. That winter we
spent in a tin caravan. The condensation used to freeze. Back in those
days, even though the pub had burnt down, Mum still ran the pub
from a lean-to. Dad was a rat catcher. He had all the traps and used to
poison moles as well. As children we had to pick up the worms in a tin
for bait, out on the fields after ploughing behind the tractor. We had to
fight off the seagulls. He got a shilling for squirrel tails. Before that he
was in the Air Force during the war. I never knew my grandfather, but
my great-great-grandfather was a stonemason and helped restore the
tower on Beaminster Church. Originally we are from Loders. We've
always worked with our hands.

Mother's side are farmers. They owned a farm at Misterton and
Granddad had a calf place at the turn of the century and was
exporting calves to America on sailing ships. He bought and sold
cattle on the Chicago markets. My auntie has a photo of him in a top
hat and tailcoat with a gun in his holster. He came back in 1915.
Granddad died in 1950 aged ninety, so he was born in 1860 and when
he was talking about cowboys and Indians he meant the real thing. He
used to smoke a pipe, wore black and had a fat tummy.

A few years ago my brother spotted a picture in Oscar's when it
was an antique shop and it was of our family in Misterton, stood

outside, so he bought it for a fiver. Others would have just had it for the frame. I was brought up in the pub till I was sixteen and never been out of one since. After The New Inn we went to The Crown in Lopen. We had three bedrooms we used upstairs and in the fourth we kept chickens. Brother still hatches out chickens in his kitchen. Beer all came in wooden barrels. We had blue lias floors.

That night the house burnt down it was raining very hard and our bonfire was aborted. The boys had hoppers or jumping jacks as they are called today and would throw them down on the flagstones. In the end it was a rocket from the churchyard opposite. It exploded in the thatch. We were left with nothing. We couldn't get the wardrobes down the stairs and the furniture we could get out got soaked in the car park. There was no mains water and so the customers formed a human chain of buckets up a ladder onto the roof. The fire brigade arrived too late.

When I did start work, I made pyjamas at Bonsoir in Crewkerne. But I got the sack after a year or two for being a bit of a rebel. It's still there. Traditional pyjamas, 4/6d for two dozen men's pyjamas, and 3/4d for children's. We had to sew the cuffs, the bottom turn-ups of the trousers and the waistband. Then I went to Clark's in Ilminster for twenty years. Machine stitching shoes. Became a shop steward. Militant I was, then they promoted me to supervisor to keep me quiet. Piece work. £14 a week. Ever-so good money then. When I went on the staff I was on £16 a week. I was twenty-four. I still dream about it now. The pressure of being boss. It's the speed. Piecework is fair, they'd be on £500 a week now if it had continued. But they kept changing the system of payment. A friend of mine still works there designing shoes to be made abroad. I took my redundancy. They wanted me to work in Street but I couldn't do the travelling. By then I was looking after twenty to fifty girls. I'd got a horse by then and started selling junk and had a stall in Bridport market and Yeovil. Never made much money out of it.

Then I took up decorating and I've been doing that sixteen, seventeen years. I just got on and done it. Decorating and gardening. I got fed up with digging. Only had two weeks without work in all that time. I did the whole of the George Hotel in Crewkerne eight years ago, Barrington Court, East Lambrook Manor, Mid Lambrook. I've even been to France and painted a house in the Dordogne. I've got a young chap with me some of the time. Just been doing a house in Petherton just behind the church. It got flooded. I enjoy doing it. In the summer I wear a bikini top and shorts. I love the sun, and performing on carnival floats. Then in winter I go hunting with the Seavington. Once they even allowed me to take my horse into The Dinnington Docks.

Five years ago I went into the *Yellow Pages* as a painter and decorator and I am still the only woman in there. I like working for myself. You can have your lunch when you want to.

'The idea is to have fun'
Catherine Pike - Joint Master of West Country Bloodhounds,
North Perrott

I was born in Oadby in Leicestershire and grew up in Bournemouth.
Parents were hoteliers. I was there from six till early twenties. I liked it.
I used to ride in the New Forest. I'd go to a riding school at Burley
Manor. I bought my first horse when I got my first job. A computer
company on Poole Quay. My father's father was a Metropolitan
policeman in London, he came down from Berwick to look for work.
My father's house in Edgware was bombed during the war and they
survived by sheltering under the kitchen table. My grandmother
worked cleaning for a Jewish family in Golders Green and then in a
stocking factory. My mother's father was in the Royal Marine Police in
Portsmouth and then got sent to Mombasa. My mother was born at
Cowes on the Isle of Wight, and during the war was evacuated to
Exmoor. They lived on the harb's farm, he's the one who identified the
stags and picked them out when they had to be culled or hunted. Mum
then moved to London and worked in Richard Henry's La-di-da Hair
Salon as a receptionist in Sloane Square.

  After Poole Quay my parents sold their hotel in Bournemouth, Pine
Beach on the edge of the chine on the Boscombe side, and came to The
Bent Tree restaurant on the A30. They wanted to cut down a bit and I
worked there for them, waitress and bar work, front of house, till I met
Nigel, the local farrier. He used to shoe my horse, he didn't charge me...
so that was a bit of a giveaway, but he charges me now, fourteen years
down the line... So I settled here in North Perrott. I found work in

Yeovil - G.F. Banbury, Fruit and Veg Merchants Wholesale. Service manager's secretary, in charge of the lorry fleet. Twenty-five thirty-eight-ton lorries. Refrigerated. We made sure they started. Then I moved to Mercedes Benz Commercial. Two years there as receptionist. Then I had my daughter Shanna. When she was about a year old we started the pack of bloodhounds.

There's only about a dozen other packs in the country and there's three or four in Ireland. This is the only one in the West Country. The nearest are in Oxfordshire and Sussex. Only two are in private ownership. Bloodhounds have been traced back to the 7th century AD where they were formed in France by Francois Hubert. Packs of St Hubert's hounds came over in 1066 with William the Conqueror. In the 16th century bloodhounds were found to be too slow and were bred with greyhounds to speed them up and again in the 1960s with Dumfriesshire foxhound. It was very popular on the Continent. Bloodhounds are very different to draghounds who follow an artificial scent.

We started off with four hounds and had a litter every year. We kept most of them. A mixed pack. We go to a different destination every Sunday. Pack them up on the lorry and drive off. On the day before, we take the runner out and show him where to stop and start, which are the right farms, where the roads and lakes are, the deep ditches. We travel most of Dorset. Weymouth, Cerne Abbas, Ashley Chase, Marshwood Vale, Cricket St Thomas, Hardington Vale and Bridport town centre on Boxing Day. Bloodhounds have always hunted on Sundays. We do three miles of line, and maybe do three or four lines a day. The runner is unpaid and leaves twenty minutes beforehand leaving behind a t-shirt, not too sweaty, it's the musk that they follow and it's better with a fit person. The hounds are controlled by the hunt staff, Whippers-In. The Huntsman has a horn. The Whippers-In wear black and we wear scarlet. Once unloaded we walk them down the road. Ten and a half couple and we have a field of anything between ten and fifty on horseback. All sorts. Some hunt six days a week and come to us on the seventh. Others work at Tesco's. The man runs with a pound or two of sausages. A Value pack cooked and chopped as a reward. The idea is to have fun. It is not a race or a competition. People pay £20 a meet. There are no subscriptions. We advertise in *The Western Gazette* and there is a Supporters Club. We hope to have about twenty-five meets between October and March, but it's been so wet this year I daren't ask the farmers to ride over their land.

I do find it bloody hard work, and I do the secretarial side of it and the accounts. I have also started working in Crewkerne with a computer firm, preparing medical files for scanning on to CDs. It's very enjoyable, it's warm, dry and I get paid...

I'll keep doing the bloodhounds till Shanna takes over.

'You get to know your fore-quarter from your topside'
Sandra Pocock — Butcher, Crewkerne

I was born in Northampton. My dad worked at Ford's Motor
Company and my mum worked in the local chemist's. It was a village
called Long Buckby between Rugby and Northampton. My mum's
dad was a grocer, he worked in the local Co-op. My other granddad
was born near Swindon. He was a groom and my gran was in service.
She was a cook and used to work for the lord of the manor. They moved
to Cattistock, he was looking after horses. Then they moved up north
to Butby Wharf on the Grand Union Canal. Granddad then went to
work in a light engineering firm and Gran worked for Golden Wonder
crisps. Prior to that she worked in The Blue Boar, one of the first
service stations on the M1 at the Watford Gap. That must have been
early 1960s.

   Myself? I left school in 1974 and got a job in Baxter's the butchers. I
was sixteen and I worked there for eight years on the administration in
head office. Personnel department... paper shuffling. They had 850
shops and this was the big HQ. The abattoir was down the road. I met
my first husband Barry over the phone. He was a District Manager
covering the Bournemouth area and next time he came up we went out
for a meal. That was 1981. Got married in 1982. Barry was very
outspoken and said something to the Personnel Manager and got
demoted and sent to Fleet. But he had a friend in Weymouth who told
us about a butcher's shop for sale in Crewkerne. We moved in on June
3rd 1982 and opened on Monday 7th June. No meat, not a bloody
thing. Terrifying. Handling meat, handling customers. All very

daunting, didn't know a pork chop from a lamb chop. Into the unknown. Something I had never done before. We all need a challenge. You get to know your fore-quarter from your topside!

It was physically very hard work. Open by seven o'clock. Things were pretty tight to start with. Every bit of money we had went into the business. As an extra we made sausages for Mr While, who sold them at Gateway's in Cheltenham. We made about half a ton a week. We also used to cure our own bacon with polka salt and Demerara. We lived above the shop and sometimes worked till two o'clock in the morning. We would get through three or four sides of beef a week. We also had a deli counter with cheese. On the floor we had sawdust, an old-fashioned parquet floor. That was difficult to keep clean. We then had tiles put down. My job was also to make homemade pies. We had homemade faggots and burgers, cooked and cured our own ham, and had roast beef, roast pork and roast chickens.

BSE... that was the worst, mismanaged thing I have ever come across. I felt sorry for the farmers. So what with Chernobyl, Edwina Currie, foul pest, swine fever and now foot and mouth, where does it all end? Sales of beef went down a bit, but then patriotism took over... mince and burgers were hit hard. Now we trace all the animals and we always know where they come from. No foreign meat, just Aberdeen Angus. In 1988 we celebrated the centenary of Barrett Bros who started the business in 1888.

Eighteen years I was in that shop. I've got the mouth for it. You chat to the customers. Ask if the daughter's still got the chicken pox, how's the husband? Kick the dog and pat the kids, or is it the other way round? Depends how well you know them. You just had to show a polite interest without overstepping the mark. But sometimes I did want to know more...

Sadly Barry died in 1993 and the people of Crewkerne were absolutely brilliant. I had 120 sympathy cards. I carried on till the end of last year, partly for therapy reasons. Then I realised I needed a change. Looking for something else to do. I knew my job inside out. I was over forty. I needed a challenge.

My present husband is a builder. His father is a Shepherd near Merriott, Mike Flatt, who always gets prizes for his Dorset Horns. I now live in Yeovil and have a new job. I work for Herbert White the Jewellers in Princes Street. Posh, up-market job. Less hours. Lovely. Nine to five, four days a week. And it's warm. I can sit down. Selling diamond rings, not tripe and chitterlings. They're a bit more security conscious. I have to look smart, a skirt, not jeans and jumper. Totally different, can't use the cheek, have to watch my language. Can't say shit... Different clientele... Lords and ladies, silver toothpicks... Come home smelling of perfume. That's different... There's more to life than work.

Afterword

The idea for this project came to me several years ago when I was involved with performance readings of verbatim statements taken from the Poor Law Commissioners' reports for 1843 and 1867. These statements from farmworkers' wives left a deep impression and I wanted to find out how things were for working women in the countryside today.

Then Pauline Rook received financial backing from South West Arts through the Year of the Artist to produce photographic portraits of thirty Somerset women for an exhibition called 'Hands On'. Further support from Somerset Now! and the Somerset Rural Life Museum in Glastonbury enabled me to interview all the women and take down their words to form a series of verbatim statements to be displayed alongside the pictures in the exhibition. I also made digital recordings of the women speaking. These are now stored in the museum.

This book was printed with the help of the Paul Hamlyn Foundation and its purpose is to form a permanent printed record of the project.

Researching *Working Women of Somerset* has been an exciting and revealing journey into personal histories, hard graft and rural attitudes. We have been very privileged to enter people's homes and listen to their reminiscences.

I hope that these black and white photographs and brief life histories will be seen as a tribute to the continuing work, skill and ingenuity of women who choose to make their living in the countryside.

James Crowden

Pauline Rook, ARPS, grew up in the countryside with a passion for photography. After a university eduation she married and moved to Somerset where she assisted her husband in the running of a large dairy farm. She now lives in Lopen and has further developed her photographic practice to include portraiture. Her photographs have been exhibited widely across the South West, she has a regular photographic feature in *The Somerset Magazine* and her work has been published in national magazines. *Working Women of Somerset* is her second book – her first, *Bridgwater – The Parrett's Mouth*, also with James Crowden, was praised for providing a unique insight into the Bridgwater area.

James Crowden was born in 1954 and grew up on the western edge of Dartmoor. He joined the Army, read civil engineering at Bristol University, and then in 1976 hightailed it to the Himalayas. Afterwards, he studied anthropology at Oxford before returning to Bristol and working in the docks as a boatman. He then spent twenty years as an agricultural labourer doing sheep shearing, night lambing, forestry work and cidermaking. Crowden has since retired from the land to concentrate on his writing and lives in Winsham in South Somerset. His other books are *Blood, Earth and Medicine* (1991), *In Time of Flood – The Somerset Levels – The River Parrett* (1996), *Cider – The Forgotten Miracle* (1999) an account of cidermaking and its history, *Bridgwater – The Parrett's Mouth* (2000), a collection of poems and notes, plus photographs by Pauline Rook, and *The Wheal of Hope – South Crofty and Cornish Tin Mining* (2000), with photographs by George Wright.

ABOUT AGRE BOOKS

Agre Books is a small, independent publisher that specialises in non-fiction books about South West subjects. Based in Dorset, it covers the South West peninsula.

Agre takes its name from the legend of Actaeon and Diana as told in Ovid's *Metamorphoses*. Ovid names Actaeon's hounds and lists their attributes. 'The thicket searcher Agre' was the hound with the keenest nose. Agre Books searches the thickets of its distinctly rural region to find interesting truths and intriguing stories.

To find out more about Agre you can write to Agre Books, Groom's Cottage, Nettlecombe, Bridport, Dorset, DT6 3SS. You can read extracts from books and discover more about Agre's authors by visiting the website at www.agrebooks.co.uk.

A SELECTION OF OTHER AGRE TITLES

The Cornish Pasty by Stephen Hall (£4.99). An illustrated and entertaining account of the original fast food. Includes authentic recipes, old postcards, new cartoons and a wealth of information sure to delight anyone interested in food and Cornwall.

For Love of Williamina by Ralph Rochester (£6.99). Williamina was loved by poet Sir Walter Scott, but she spurned him. In 1810 she fell ill and travelled to Lympstone. This charming, romantic book gives an unsurpassed picture of late-Georgian Devon.

Islomania (£6.50) by Sara Hudston with photographs from the Gibson Archive on the Isles of Scilly. Islomania - an overwhelming obsession with islands. Why are islands so captivating? This book explores islomania using Scilly as its main example.

The Wheal of Hope (£9.99). Poems and notes by James Crowden, photographs by George Wright. The closure of South Crofty tin mine marked the end of 3,000 years of history. Wright and Crowden record the mine's final months.

ABOUT THE PRINTING OF THIS BOOK

Working Women of Somerset was typeset by Agre Books in Monotype Classic Octavian. The cover was designed by Stuart Brill at Senate Design Ltd in London. The book was printed and bound on 130gsm art paper by R. Booth (Bookbinders) Ltd of Mabe, near Penryn in Cornwall, a small family firm founded in 1971.